BETTER OR BITTER MEN

BY

HOMER L. GOOD
And
CORT R. FLINT

INTRODUCTION
BY
NORMAN VINCENT PEALE

DROKE HOUSE, *Publishers*
ANDERSON, S. C.

Distributed By
GROSSET & DUNLAP
51 Madison Avenue, New York, N. Y.

BETTER MEN OR BITTER MEN

Copyright © 1969 By Homer L. Good and Cort R. Flint

All Rights Reserved. No part of this book may be reproduced or transmitted in any form or by any means, electronic or mechanical, including photocopying, or by any information storage or retrieval system, without permission in writing from the publisher.

FIRST EDITION

Standard Book Number: 8375-6740-8
Library of Congress Catalog Card Number: 70-79402

Published by DROKE HOUSE, Publishers, Inc.
Anderson, S. C.

MANUFACTURED IN THE UNITED STATES OF AMERICA

BOOK DESIGN BY LEWIS N. SCHILLING, JR.

THIS BOOK IS DEDICATED TO

S. H. Mitchell, President

and

Vice-Presidents

W. Ned Mitchell

J. L. Phipps

Hennis Freight Lines, Winston-Salem, North Carolina

*whose vision, ingenuity, concern
and generosity have made possible
this book and its contents.*

TABLE OF CONTENTS

I.	"Through A Glass Clearly"	10
II.	"Lovely Nancy"	17
III.	"But For The Grace of God"	25
IV.	"Nobody Gives A Damn"	48
V.	"Upon Reaching The Golden Age"	56
VI.	"Why Did Daddy Kill Himself?"	62
VII.	"The Hell You Say!"	68
VIII.	"I Just Go In Circles"	79
IX.	"Dear Chaplain"	85
X.	"You Don't Have To Stay As You Are"	110
XI.	"These Damn Conflicts"	122
XII.	"Can I Ever Live Again?"	130
XIII.	"Is There A Pill?"	135
XIV.	"Understanding Your Dreams"	142
XV.	"Everybody Is Against Me"	153
XVI.	"Better Men Or Bitter Men"	160
XVII.	"I'm Sure Glad I Did"	166
XVIII.	"God Is Not Dead After All"	171
XIX.	"She's So Tough"	176
XX.	"Checking Yourself Out For Action"	183

INTRODUCTION

This interesting book is written by two industrial Chaplains with whose excellent work I am familiar. They are ministers working, not as pastors of churches, but rather as spiritually motivated friends of the men and women connected with a large business enterprise.

Mr. Shirley Mitchell, president of Hennis Freight Lines of Winston-Salem, North Carolina, is an enlightened industrialist who has a strong personal concern for his workers and who possesses a sense of responsibility for his men and their families. Accordingly, he was one of the first to establish in his company the position of Industrial Chaplain. He also created in the main offices a beautiful Chapel, which I had the privilege of dedicating several years ago. Both the Chapel and the Chaplains are dedicated to the human service of all who are connected with this far-flung enterprise.

Mr. Mitchell's trucks operate in the southern, eastern, and midwestern states, and as far west as Denver, Colorado. Often the driver will visit the Chapel before rolling out on a long-distance trip. And if any trouble strikes in their families while they are absent the Chaplains are present to help and to reach the driver himself with a supportive ministry wherever he may be.

In any great organization all the usual human problems are present, for wherever there are people the problems that beset mankind are always to be found. Many of the employees are of course members of churches and turn to their own pastors in time of trouble. But often the Industrial Chaplain can fill a special need due to his unique working relationship to the worker. However, the Chaplain and the local pastor often team up in dealing with personal and family problems. The non-clerical or non-churchly character of the Chaplain's position often inspires confidences that might not be given to the pastor of one's church. That the skilled and dedicated Industrial Chaplain has a function of extraordinary importance in contemporary American society is evidenced by this fascinating book written by experts in this field.

The book is filled with down-to-earth case histories of persons whose problems were alleviated and brought to creative solution through the insights and love and wise helpfulness of Industrial Chaplains. The rehabilitative skill of the Chaplain is revealed in the making of better men and correspondingly better workers.

I recommend the book especially to industrialists who desire more effective and positive relations with their people. Pastors and counselors will find the book extremely valuable for its documented case history studies. And the average reader may find his own problem mirrored in the stories of others and thereby be guided to insight and understanding that will prove personally helpful.

This is a splendid book that ought to do much good in spreading the hopeful message that there is an answer for any human problem when creative treatment is brought to it.

NORMAN VINCENT PEALE

PREFACE

The industrial chaplain fills a unique need in business relationships and in the overall planning of the goals in industry. It is an established fact that men will either become better or bitter according to their reactions to their environment, work, home, church, and opportunities to live at the highest each day.

One man has the best position to help those who aspire to become better men – those who take the indications of their dissatisfactions to be a God-given barometer that a more meaningful life can be obtained. A chaplain is with people where they work and becomes a part of that great team-play which has made the American businessman and his employees the examples for other parts of the world. Books are now being written in foreign nations calling upon business leaders to use the policies of industrial leaders in the United States of North America.

This special place that the chaplain has in being a vital part of both management and labor gives him a means of serving which no one has ever had. He is on a first name basis with the top executives, those who perform what may be described as the most menial tasks, and with those in between.

The word gets around to everyone that the chaplain is one person who will take time to listen. He is concerned about all people in all circumstances. Problems that may seem minor are as important as those that are major. The reason. . . . the human personality is at stake anytime that an individual shares his heart's concern. Listening intensely to the person talk out his concern brings to him his deepest desire – to be understood – for someone to hear him – to find a sense of direction for his life.

Those who have been in places of leadership and those who have faced themselves, have learned the great truth that everybody needs somebody to care for him. and to listen to him. The greater the intellect, the more guidance a man needs in his emotional life. A man's higher intellectual capacity causes him to rationalize about his emotions and he never confronts himself. The old saying, "He should know better", just won't hold water. Most people do as they feel. By having a better understanding of himself man can do a better job of guiding his feelings.

Much gratitude is expressed to those who are sharing their lives in this book. The names have been changed in most instances except in the special chapters.

They have shared their heartaches, depressions, sorrows, successes, and how they found their way through the dark places. Only a small portion of their experiences is told. The background of how the information was obtained is omitted. Anyone of these people could, if the details were given, fill a book. They have bared themselves to the public so that someone traveling the same road may realize that there is hope for everyone. Such aid does not usually come in the manner a person expects. It is in the willingness to turn loose of an old life to attempt a new one that all the great discoveries have been made. Jesus taught that man must lose his life in order to find it. To turn loose of life under man's own control to begin another life that has different structures and new knowledge is never easy. There are those who start and then become afraid and return to the old patterns of behavior, misery, and fears. They hide from life rather than enter into life. They believe their misery is safe even though it is not compatible.

The chaplain is much more of an instrument, a channel through which help can flow, than he is the source of help.

In a low-key way this book endeavors to bring into focus these facts:

1. God is more willing to hear His children than we are to communicate with Him.

2. God is anxious to extend His love to all who will seek it.

3. Divine forgiveness is always ours if we will but seek it.

4. Everyone can have meaning to his life.

This is not a scholarly work seeking to describe in technical terms the treatment of human ills which everyone faces in varying degrees. It is a down to earth sharing of people as they have learned to reveal themselves. The hope of the authors is that each reader will go back again and again to the chapters to find inspiration and help to make each day more joyful and significant.

Many who read these pages are so determined to have a better life instead of a bitter life, that they will risk their necks and their lives in order to live. The authors' prayers and deep concern will be with each reader. Every man will be a victor instead of a victim.

Everyone can learn how to let God live in him each day... how to be God's man in all human relationships... how to be a participant in human relations and religious groups and to accept the responsibility of being a hospital administering spiritual love and concern for all people.

Homer L. Good
Cort R. Flint

CHAPTER I

"THROUGH A GLASS – CLEARLY"

The world is full of fools; and he who would not wish to see one, must not only shut himself up alone, but must also break his looking glass.
— Boileau

Life that ever needs forgiveness has for its first duty to forgive.
— Bulwer

The greatest difficulty is to forgive self.

It is a tight rope that must be walked by the industrial Chaplain. In fact, his career is marked by many tight ropes. His greatest reward is when, in dealing with delicate human emotions and deepest personal problems, he can negotiate the distance from one platform to another on the far end of the rope without stumbling. Because just as surely as the circus performer will fall if he stumbles badly, the Chaplain will fail miserably if, in traversing the unknown depths of misery in the lives of those he seeks to help, he takes a false step. Just as the aerialist finds some wires tauter than others, the chaplain finds in some of his charges emotions so complex they seem to defy penetration.

This was the situation with Bob. His family owned a large share of the industry which now benefited from his drive and aggressiveness. He was successful in getting from his subordinates the same kind of productiveness he demanded of himself and the same dedication he felt to the company. He held the highest office his church could bestow upon a layman; he quickly achieved posts of leadership in every civic organization with which he affiliated. By any yardstick Bob's public life had to be considered highly successful. But the most superficial examination from afar of Bob's accomplishments would reveal to the trained observer that there was great volatility in this man. His relationships with others were always marked with the greatest possible detachment; he was sharp, defensive – obviously driven by just one desire, to get the job done. It was plain that he found no joy in his accomplishments. It was clear that some trouble burned almost out of control in this man.

Penetrating Bob's shell was like trying to open an oyster with a toothpick. It was clear to the Chaplain after several visits to him that Bob would not talk. Offers of help were couched in the most delicate terms and made in the most indirect fashion because it was obvious that Bob would tolerate no prying into his affairs for any reason whatsoever.

But the Chaplain, in his lowest possible key, persisted with periodic visits. Then late on a day that had been an unusually severe challenge to Bob, he suddenly, and possibly without realizing it, exploded "I can't face it, I can't face it, I just can't face it any longer."

"What is it that you can't face; what is bothering you, burning in you so hard?" asked the Chaplain.

"Well, it was twenty years ago. I had been ruled all my life by my dominating parents. I was forty years old then, and had worked half those years right here in this plant, seeing it grow from a small undertaking to the big industry it was even then. But my father made all the decisions, gave all the orders, — had no use for or confidence in my suggestions for doing even better with the business. Then he died. My mother told me then that from that time on I was to make the decisions. But almost immediately I began to run across instances almost every day where she had stepped in before me and given instructions, stated policy on company affairs I thought I was supposed to be running. I felt that I wasn't appreciated or needed here. At home it seemed that my wife didn't appreciate me, even though I had provided well for her and the kids. My sex life suffered and I came to look on myself as something less than a man.

"I began to find comfort here at the plant where there was a young woman working close to me who seemed to be interested in what I was doing and how it was being done. Her expressions of interest and her compliments to me picked me up. I began to think of her as being the only person in the world who had any confidence in me. She was younger than I and very attractive. I began to feel that in her eyes at least I was somebody and that maybe I did have something on the ball even if my family didn't think so. Our affair quickly grew to enormous proportions — too big to continue around here. So we pulled up and went to New York to live together in the obscurity that great city offered. I had money enough of my own for us to live on and it seemed that everything would then be alright. This young woman had obviously not been promiscuous prior to my finding her; she had been lonely and looking for some way to make her life more meaningful. Yes, everything was alright except for one thing, *my conscience.*

"My need for reassurance as to my manhood was very adequately met; her need for a sense of security was satisfied. But with each passing day I became more and more miserable. Pretty soon I knew there was only one thing to do and that was to call the whole thing off.

"So, after six months of life with her in New York I came back to face the music here. My family's financial interest made re-employment here a certainty. My wife put her forgiveness into words and took me back. My pastor assured me of his forgiveness and promised that the people of my church would, in time, forgive and forget.

"Well, twenty years have passed. Many of the people here who knew about my escapade have died or moved away. If I could accept their attitudes at face value I would believe that the rest of the townspeople have, indeed, accepted the prodigal's return with forgiveness and thanksgiving. Yet, I am so filled with hate for myself, disgust and frustration I don't know which way to turn. The only relief I can find is in total immersion in my work. And that is only partial relief. I feel that if I let my guard down somebody will get close enough to me to castigate me for something I did 20 years ago, even though I have castigated myself every single day for it. So I give everybody short shrift; I'm not about to let anybody get close to me. And I ought to have my head examined for talking to you this way. It's none of your affair. What's been done is done. Talking about it now isn't going to do any good. There's only one thing for me to do and that's to keep on the course I've followed for 20 years until I do go off my rocker and they cart me off from here in a straight jacket."

Bob was obviously drained by this exposure of his inner feelings. After an interval the Chaplain said "There is something that will do some good, and you have just done it. Getting this thing out in the open is the first step. I won't try to minimize the seriousness of what happened 20 years ago. But you have been far too hard on yourself all these years. The kind of life you have lived since returning here certainly has gone a long way toward redeeming you in the eyes of your fellow workers and the townspeople. The important thing now is to treat with the scars you have inflicted on your own soul since you decided to do the right thing and return here to your prime responsibilities. This I want to help you with. But enough has been said for this time. You go on home and try to relax a little and I'll see you again tomorrow."

Late the next day the chaplain dropped in on Bob again. When the last of the other employees had left Bob again spoke.

"You know, I have attended some of those human relations groups you've been leading. I remember what you have said about self-preservation being the strongest human instinct. Do you think it might have been this instinct surfacing in me that prompted my behavior 20 years ago?"

"Yes," said the Chaplain. "That, and the second strongest instinct, the sexual drive, the deep, oftentimes unrecognized need for an outlet for adequate sexual expression. Unfortunately, there are many times when both of these emotions become confused with some other problems. Have you wondered whether the conditions under which you lived and labored may have given rise to some other problems? I can see where the frustrations of a domineering parent who countermanded your authority could have suggested to your subconscious mind that your existence and position as head of the company were being threatened."

Bob thought for a long time. Then he answered, "That might be. Carrying the thought a little further, it might also be that what I thought then was a threat to my manhood, even a denial to my manhood, was just an extenuation of conditions arising from my mother's subjugation of my authority. Neither she nor my wife were ever close enough to my performance arena to know whether or not I was doing my job well. Mother's changes in my own management direction gave little opportunity to see the finished result of my ideas. When this girl came so fully into my life and eventually offered me an outlet for my frustrations and new sex opportunities I think perhaps all my problems balled themselves into what I viewed as a threat to my own preservation. She gave me the compliments I never got anywhere else. Along with it was an uninhibited sexual outlet. There may have been other reasons for my defection but they all led back to these two principal causes."

"Yes," responded the Chaplain. "And from what you have told me, there was anger in your heart that your authority to run the company was being rendered impotent. There must have been some fear, too. Not many men pass the dangerous years of their early forties without some fear that they have reached the years of their maximum production without accomplishing what they think they should have. So you had both anger and fear. They often breed hate. Anger, fear and hate precipitated in you the need for defensive action. And now, today, you are letting yourself be perfectly miserable by the consequence of that action. Unfortunately, you may be magnifying that misery by your refusal to face facts as they really are."

"That," said Bob, "is the silliest thing you could have possibly said. For twenty years I have seen reproach in the faces of people around here for what I did a long time ago. For twenty years I have felt the reproof of people I see everyday. I learned a long time ago to head these people off before they have a chance to go to work on me. This is my defense. And it has been hell. What I want to know is what can I do about it."

"Bob," said the Chaplain, "You are confusing defense with acceptance. One of the hardest things a man can do is to accept the things he cannot change. You cannot change one single detail of what happened more than 20 years ago. To your everlasting credit, you did another one of the hardest things; you came back here and admitted that you had done wrong. You asked forgiveness of your pastor, your fellow churchmen, your fellow townsmen and your wife and family. From all I have ever been able to learn, you have been granted forgiveness in all these quarters. I have been around here for a while, and I have heard the confidences of more people than you would believe. But do, please, believe me when I say to you that these mere mortals have forgiven you. I can't deny that some isolated individuals with cesspools for minds may have been unwilling to forget entirely that you made a mistake. But these same people have catalogued in their minds every mistake they ever heard of anybody in this town making. Had they lived 2000 years ago they would have been among those who cast lots for the Lord's garments."

There were several more conferences with Bob, and with each one his burden seemed to grow a little lighter. He seemed more willing to talk and spoke more freely. Then one day he told the Chaplain what the Chaplain already knew but felt should come from Bob's own lips.

"Chaplain," he said, "I might have figured this thing out if I didn't first go insane. But it was you who has, in these conferences day after day, so patiently sowed in my mind the seeds that have produced my conclusions.

"I have dropped my armor a little in the past few weeks just to see if there was any substance to what you said about the forgiveness of people. Early in our discussions we carefully, and I think accurately, analyzed the reasons for my disgraceful conduct a long time ago. I had pretty well figured that one out for myself anyway. What was really bothering me was what I thought the people were still saying and thinking and what they would do to me if they ever had a chance. But recently I have been testing them a little. And do you know, I think they have really forgiven and mostly forgotten. The trouble is that I never accepted their forgiveness. More importantly, I asked God twenty years ago to forgive me and I have asked Him every day since to forgive me. What has been so hellish for me is that in my preoccupation with my own emotions it has never occurred to me until the last few days that God has forgiven me. More importantly, I have not accepted His forgiveness. I have not accepted His goodness. I have not accepted the hundreds of opportunities He has given me for what they were: chances to redeem myself in His eyes and in the eyes of my fellowmen. I took on every job the church offered me, every assignment given me by the Kiwanis Club, Community Chest, Chamber of Commerce, in order to deprive those people of any chance they might have to resurrect the mistakes of my past life. I finished those jobs as fast and as well as I could and in as much 'lone wolf' manner as possible in order to keep people from ever having a chance to get to me. All these jobs and assignments — they were just chances for me to pay the rent for the space I occupy on this good earth. They were given me as gestures by the people and assurances by my God that I have, indeed, been forgiven.

"I have for years refused to accept the love of my wife and family because I didn't think I was worthy of it. But God does not deal with us according to our iniquities; He deals with us out of His everlastingly abundant love for us.

"You didn't perform any miracles, Chaplain. You just led me to unlock my heart to the goodness of God, His forgiveness, and the compassion of friendship people around me have offered through the years when I was too stubborn to accept it. Thank you, Chaplain, and forgive me further if I trespass on your territory and say with all my heart, "God bless you."

Bob's experiences illustrate how difficult it is to accept forgiveness, love, and a lease on a new life.

If you are facing a similar situation, practice these suggestions:

1. God will forgive me. Forgiveness is seeing what is wrong in my life and seeking God's means of transformation.

2. I will forgive myself and practice loving myself as Jesus taught. I realize the attitude I take toward myself will be reflected in my attitude toward others.

3. I will receive love and give love to the best of my ability and capacity each day.

4. I will fill my heart with beautiful thoughts and seek to grow in my capacities for love and understanding.

5. God wants me to have a meaningful life. I will accept it.

6. Sex is an important phase in anyone's life. I will learn to recognize this drive and bring it to its place in my life. This will apply to the normal and beautiful life with my marriage mate. It will also be in transmuting the sex drive to worthy endeavors in life. The latter will develop creativeness in me.

7. I will eliminate the negative and accentuate the positive.

CHAPTER II

"LOVELY NANCY"

A man should never be ashamed to confess he has been wrong, which is but saying, in other words, that he is wiser today than he was yesterday.
— *Pope*

Confession is the first beginning of good works.
— *Augustine*

Depression comes, not from having faults, but from the refusal to face them.
— *Fulton J. Sheen*

The services and counsel of the chaplain are not available only to the employees of the plant; guests and salesmen calling at the plant sometimes seek him out and customers have found comfort by talking to the plant chaplain. A major part of the chaplain's responsibility is in caring for the families of plant employees. Effective counseling in the case of an employee experiencing domestic difficulties can be accomplished only if conferences can be had with both the husband and the wife. There have been cases in which the chaplain has counseled with entire families. Most often, however, when other family members are brought to the chaplain's attention it is because a mother or father asks if a child might drop by and talk. Thus it was that the chaplain came to meet lovely Nancy Emerson.

Nancy was very much on the defensive as she entered his office. Experience had taught him to expect this attitude when a youngster visits him as the result of great pressure brought by a parent. Unfortunately, in such cases it is often a last ditch effort to try to bring some order into a young life before it becomes necessary to let law enforcement authorities or the courts take over. Knowing this, the young man or woman is usually possessed of whatever attitude he or she believes to comprise the best defense. Nancy was no exception.

"I guess my mother has drawn a great big horrible picture of me," she began when pleasantries had been exchanged. "She just doesn't understand people younger than she is. What makes her think you do? For that matter what makes *you* think you can tell other people how to live?"

"Wait just a minute, there," he said. "I've never told anybody that I can tell them how to live."

"Well, what's the pitch then? What makes you any better than anybody else? What gives you the right to sit in judgment on me? How come you think you can tell me whether I am right or wrong? What makes you so great?"

"Nancy," he said, "You have come in here with a lot of preconceived notions that are not founded on fact. Chaplains or preachers, or rabbis or priests or pastors — whatever you want to call them, are not neccessarily any better than anybody else, not even when they wear their collars backwards. But automobile mechanics are trained to hear if a motor is not performing just right. Doctors are trained to hear the heart and identify any malfunction audible in that organ. Chaplains are trained to just listen. As far as I personally am concerned, I have studied psychology in order to learn the behavioural sciences; I have worked with psychiatrists who have studied the hows and whys of certain forms of behaviour and made a science out of finding corrective procedures where necessary. And I have studied the ministry in order to learn more of how our God expects us to live our lives, and to learn more about interpreting God's will for those who have not had the theological insight of ministerial students. None of this makes me any better than anybody else; none of it guarantees that I can even give you an answer, or that my answer will be right. But the most important thing is that I have learned to listen real well. And when I hear what you have to say, I will first try very hard to put myself in your place and examine what you say from that view point before looking at your problem from any other angle."

Nancy thought for a moment and said, "Well, if I tell you anything at all about what mother says is my problem you will do just like she did; raise hell with me. And I've had enough of that."

"Nancy, I promise you that whatever you tell me, somebody else has told me something as bad or worse. And whatever is on your mind and whatever you tell me about it I will not raise hell. I will only try to act as an instrument through which God can speak. He and I together will try to help you; not fuss at you. But the only way you will ever know is to try me. So why don't you tell me just what brought you here."

Tears came into Nancy's eyes, just as the first trickle through a broken dam, and then her own dam against her emotions broke through and the tears came in torrents. When she had calmed down it was evident that great relief had already come to her. Apparently she decided then to see if even more relief might be forthcoming. She abandoned the belligerence and defensiveness that marked her countenance when she first came in and began to speak in a soft voice.

"My mother has always been pretty strict. In small ways I resisted her authority from the time I was very young. Something began to happen to me about four years ago – when I was fourteen – and I knew I could no longer put up with her bossiness just by answering back under my breath, or pretending that I had answered out loud. Other girls my age were beginning to have their boy friends and go to parties and have company. I got in on some of that but my mother was so much more strict than other mothers.

"I began to do spiteful things. For some reason I thought I was getting even when I lied to mother; mean, senseless lies about nothing at all, — just lying about everything. If she asked me if I walked home from school with Mary I'd tell her no, I had walked with Sue even though it had been Mary. If I had been over to Sandy's house I would tell her I had been to Karen's. Just crazy things like that. I thought it was fun to deceive her; I had a great time because I was putting something over on her.

"And then I wanted things she wouldn't buy for me, like more skirts and sweaters and things. So I started walking through stores that had the things I wanted and when nobody was looking I would grab something and hide it until I got out of the store. When mother asked me where I got these things I just told her I borrowed them from some of my girl friends. In order to keep things moving I began asking my friends to come to the house and get these things and wear them. This seemed to offer the proof I needed that I was wearing other people's clothes instead of wearing things I had stolen. She fussed at me for wearing the other girls' clothes but I kept right on stealing and then passing things around among the other girls to try to keep up the proof that I was borrowing lots of clothes.

"On the nights she would let me out of the house without too much fuss it just didn't seem like I could ever get home as early as she wanted me to. So I just started staying as late as I wanted to and slipping out about every night.

"My crowd had loose morals and I loosened mine, too because I wanted to be a part of the crowd; I couldn't stand the thought of anybody ever calling me a wet blanket. I'm ashamed to admit it but I've had about as much sex experience as anybody in the crowd.

"I was really accepted by everybody and I thought it was great. But here lately I've started thinking a lot. It's not because of what mother has said; she's said so much I haven't heard much of anything. But pretty soon I'll be 18. I graduate from high school this spring. I've been wondering where I go from here. All of a sudden life is dull and tasteless and uninteresting. The things I've been doing not only don't prepare me for marriage; they make it harder than ever for any marriage of mine to work out.

"I guess it's because I've been thinking about these things so much lately that mother got on me about coming to see you. She must have known something was bugging me. She doesn't know any of these things I've told you cause if she did I promise you she would really pop her skull. But I agreed to come see you because, in spite of my toughness when I first came in, I was getting to where I thought I was going to explode if I didn't find somebody to talk to. Oh chaplain, what am I going to do?"

"Nancy," he replied, "I don't know whether you knew it or not, but God has been sitting here with us through all our conversation. He gives us that extra understanding and strength. God is not an abstract being. He is very real. And He will give us real, meaningful help if we really want it and pray for it with sincerity and conviction. Now this has been *your* problem; it is part of *mine* now. I'll help you in every way possible. But, as I told you when you came in, I can't tell you or anybody else how to live. So you tell me how you want to live and where you want to start and we'll go on from there."

"I've been so hard headed and head strong that I've never been able to say it out loud before, but I have felt more and more lately that I really need God," replied Nancy. "Right this minute I think if I asked God to forgive me, He would wash me clean again. And I need to ask my mother's forgiveness. I'm not going to tell her all the horrible details I've been giving you because it won't do anybody any good and it would only break her heart. Can we start, chaplain, by you saying a prayer for me and helping me get started on a new life?"

"I would be glad to, Nancy, except for two things. One, I don't think one person should do all the talking and I talk to God an awful lot. Why don't you make the start by praying yourself? And let me correct you on one thing, *pray;* don't just *say* a prayer; there's a big difference."

"God, I'm glad there is a Heavenly Father who is more willing to give than are some of your children to ask. Will You now come more fully into my life; forgive me for stealing, forgive me for lying; forgive me for being a stubborn fool and forgive me for hurting others and wasting so much of Your gift of life to me. Please help me to be a better person, and let me not be such a stranger to you from this minute on. I'm sorry I've been immoral and I hope You will help me to be what You want me to be. Take my life and make something of it. Amen."

The chaplain looked at Nancy again when she had finished her little prayer. The hardness was gone from her expression. The lines of worry had been erased as if by miracle. Her eyes sparkled and it seemed that the very air was cleaner and sweeter. Before His eyes there had been a complete transformation of another human being.

And this gladness did not end there. It was revealed anew in each of the many visits Nancy paid him after that day. She became active in her church, in its youth groups and she not only left the old crowd she had associated with but managed to bring some of them with her.

Admitting one is on the wrong road is never easy. Only when there is disillusionment with life, can anyone be willing to leave one way for another. As long as a person thinks he is right or his actions are all right, he is on the defensive and unable to welcome healing and redemption.

Nancy had tired of being used by others and being a part of deception. Every act of going along with a lower standard than she really wanted brought greater dissatisfaction and unhappiness.

At first she blamed her mother's attitude and discipline. Then she came to realize that she alone was responsible for what she was. She believed she was the only one who could bring about a change. When she took a different attitude and began a life of trust, love, and respect for herself, real life began to flow in her heart again.

Everyone is moved in his behavior by his emotions. Very few have self-understanding or emotional understanding.

This adolescent change into youth is a difficult one to undergo. The psychological as well as the physical changes that take place are so radical that even the best informed and adjusted families have great difficulty. There is no easy way to get through it. Tears for mother, extra bills for daddy and revolt by a daughter or son can be expected as the normal happenings.

Counselors do not have any simple, short bits of advice or ready-made remedies about this age for parents or children. The parental aim is to be the same as the children's, to help the son or daughter develop independence and gradual emancipation from the childhood home. This requires adjustment from the parents in their attitude and management. Some adults do not want their offspring to grow up. The parents who grow with their children will help them — those who refuse to grow will hinder their children.

Two factors are important in this transition, and these are the conflicts in one's conscious opinion or attitude and the unconscious opinion or attitude. Saying yes and no to the same question troubles people all through life. It is so easy to fool self in this regard. A part of the personality says yes and a part says no. The complication grows when the conscious part says yes and the unconscious says no. But this often happens. The division of opinion is often quite transparent to other people. It is rarely evident to the victim of the conflict.

There are three levels of life to deal with in all development in the human personality. They are conscious, unconscious, and the twilight zone in between called fore-conscious. When these terms are described by comparison with light, consciousness refers to full daylight. It is closer to the surface and in nearest contact with the outside world. This is the main storehouse for working knowledge.

Below this conscious level is the twilight zone of fore-consciousness without any boundaries between. Sometimes they recall easily and at other times with difficulty or not at all.

Some make light of the influence of the unconscious level even though they are aware of the tug and pull of life. It is in this level that the experiences of childhood dwell — the information of last week and last year. The emotions that have been shoved from the conscious level are still there having their place. These have to be dealt with — the sooner the better.

Dreams are additional evidence of an unconscious level. From the unconscious life energies are gotten which are usually defined as instincts or drives. The power is a dynamic flow to every human personality rather than a limp collection of old discarded experiences or relationships.

Three other aspects of the human personality, which constantly influence lives, are the Id, the Ego and the Super-Ego. The Id is the source of instinctual energy and is limited to the region of the unconscious. The Ego makes the decisions of the will and is aware of the factors that need to be considered. It is in the conscious area but also covers the unconscious. The Super-Ego is the censor and critic. It is partly conscious but most is unconscious and functions as conscience. Since the human conscience starts early in life and is pretty well formed by the age of 8 or 10, the parents and teachers are very important. Religious training is of great value in helping to determine right and wrong. Super-Egos force people to make exaggerated efforts to pay for misdeeds out of all proportions to any damage done. Super-Ego is always prone to lay it on heavy.

How confession is used in religious faith is very essential to the well-adjusted and forgiven personality. Super-Ego holds back on forgiveness and makes one think he is not forgiven and makes great obstacles in forgiving self. Super-Ego sits on the sidelines of the fight and encounters of the Ego trying to handle the hot ones that Id is always passing on to it. When Ego tries to let some of the strivings and primitive demands of Id go out into the world in some form of behavior, Super-Ego makes Ego suffer from its disapproval. Sometimes illness is the consequence of the conflict.

Nancy had many struggles as she tried to find her way back to the life she desired. Her realization of God's love and forgiveness enabled her to find a lease on a new life.

THOUGHTS FOR CONSIDERATION

1. Rebellion about the world, parents, and the situation that youth find themselves in, is a natural response of human nature.

2. Every young person must learn how to live with human nature and how to guide his life to its best fulfillment and purpose.

3. It is best to think through patterns of behavior and choose the life that is wanted ten years from now.

4. Make decisions that can be recommended to someone else.

5. Most parents desire the best for their children even though they might be inadequate for some situations which arise.

6. Respond in love as parents and children. Each will be glad he did.

7. God's love has a way of redeeming each person who believes in Him and trusts Him for a lease on a new life.

CHAPTER III

"BUT FOR THE GRACE OF GOD....."

Drunkedness is nothing else but a voluntary madness...
— *Seneca*

Intoxicating drinks have produced evils more deadly, because more continuous, than all those caused to mankind by the great historic scourges of war, famine, and pestilence combined.
— *Gladstone*

God is our refuge and strength, an ever present help in time of trouble.
— *Psalm 46:1*

There are always those near, to be of encouragement and help.

Rick sat alone at the table in the center of his living room. Before him sat a bottle containing only a very small quantity of whiskey. The ash tray was full to overflowing, as were all the other ash trays in the room. Waste baskets hadn't been emptied in many days; newspapers from last month lay on the floor. It was a better than average apartment located in a good section of the city. But it had suffered from lack of upkeep since Esther left it some months ago.

"Was it yesterday I had that hamburger, or was it the day before," Rick asked himself. "No matter," he thought. "I couldn't swallow a bite of food if by doing so it would wipe away all that has happened these last few years."

He reached for his bottle, knowing that when this ounce or two was gone there would be no more. It was early on a beautiful spring evening. But it was Sunday and the package stores were closed. The bars sold no hard liquor on Sunday. Besides, Rick had only 73 cents to his name. The neighborhood grocery store, the laundry and the liquor store had all called in the last few days, demanding that he make good on his checks that had been returned with the notation "Insufficient Funds; do not re-deposit." As he contemplated the few remaining drops of whiskey he recalled the icy reception he had received in a similar situation three weeks earlier when he made his uncertain way to the apartments of friends in the building, hoping to be offered a drink. No use trying that again. He thought of old Leo down the block and across the street. Leo might lend him a bottle from his usual ample supply of whiskey. But, no. The last time he went on that mission Leo was a little stuffy; said something about there having been no re-payment or return made on a couple of bottles he had handed over to Rick to tide him over emergencies like this. He set the bottle down without taking a drink. Anyway, Rick doubted if he could make it to go anywhere – even for more whiskey.

It hadn't always been this way. Rick had, just five years ago, been on his way up, with a good job in a large firm that appreciated his energies, his resourcefulness, his contributions as a valuable member of the junior management team. There were no children and Esther, too, had a good job. Between them, they easily afforded this nice apartment with its attractive furniture. There was a good car and they were planning ahead for the purchase of a home of their own. Their closets were filled with good clothes and there was money in the bank. They were not of the country club set but they had many friends with whom they spent gay week-ends, at the apartment or homes of one or the other of the couples. Or they arranged house parties at the beach or in the mountains. The liquor flowed freely; a little too freely sometimes. But no real harm was done; just a little headache once in a while, which on the morning after, wore off as the day progressed.

But then things began to change for Rick. The Saturday night drinking became a more serious thing for him. It seemed that he needed more than did the other members of the party. To compensate for this need and to avoid the taunts of his friends when he took an extra drink, or two or three or a dozen more than anybody else, he began slipping to the kitchen for his extras. Or he kept an extra bottle hidden somewhere to accommodate his secret sips. The headaches of the following days became more severe and were accompanied by other strange symptoms, like extreme nervousness and shakiness and sometimes nausea. He had heard of the "hair of the dog" remedy so he treated his hangovers with increasingly generous doses of bourbon, Scotch or anything else alcoholic. This, of course, was just building fires on top of fires. Pretty soon his Saturday night indulgences carried over all day Sunday and the cures were undertaken on Mondays. It was an insidiously progressive thing. Before the year was out it was taking Rick until Wednesday to get over the previous week-end. On Thursdays he began to tune up for the approaching week-end, with the result that by the time of the Saturday night get-together, he was flying on two wings and moving full steam ahead.

As the extent of his indulgences increased, the limits of his inhibitions lessened. Rick became increasingly the captive of his moods and motivated by them. If it was gaiety, he became too exuberant. If there was any lack of gaiety he would likely sink into some deep depression. If in fact or by imagination he became offended his reaction was belligerent. Whatever the mood, he entered into it with all the enthusiasm that had drained away from application to his work.

It was only a matter of time until Esther and Rick were dropped from the old gang. Rick's antics had made it increasingly embarrassing for her to face her friends. His unpredictability and growing penchant for creating trouble, or readiness to join in on somebody else's trouble made him an undesirable.

In her bewilderment at what was happening to her husband, Esther stopped drinking with Rick or going with him to any place where liquor was likely to be served. This ostracism by his old friends — even by his wife — bothered Rick not at all. In fact, some impediments to applying himself unfettered to his drinking were removed. After work he was free to stop in bars on his way home in order to prepare himself for an evening of serious drinking. He took bottles home with him to satisfy that part of his alcoholic needs that remained after his stop-offs after work. There was no need to take time to bathe and shave and dress before going out to drink, because there was no place to go; the welcome mat had long since been removed as far as Rick was concerned. He had nothing to do but systematically empty the bottle or pass out or both.

At work, the promotions that had once come with such regularity ceased. His friends around the building avoided him more and more. One by one responsibilities were being diverted from his desk. There was no cut in pay at that time and that was providential from the point of the financial responsibilities of Rick and Esther. It had been a long time since any additions had been made to their savings. Little by little those reserves began to melt away. Even with two salaries coming in the cost of maintaining a heavy drinking habit can be enormous. The cost of the booze itself is great. An almost constant state of intoxication leads to various irresponsibilities that add to the expense of alcoholism. Like the time Rick dropped into an auction with a drinking buddy after a bout at the bar. It was pay day and instead of depositing his check as had been his former practice, Rick cashed it and put the money in his pocket. The money was needed, he reasoned, to buy his share of the rounds of drinks. Then came the auction. At the moment Rick and his buddy staggered into the room an old clock was being offered for sale. The auctioneer was ready to bang his gavel on a reasonable bid of $30 for the clock when Rick's buddy suddenly offered $35. Not to be outdone, Rick offered forty. Eventually, he paid $70 for a clock he didn't need. When they returned to the bar to further fortify themselves for their respective trips home, Rick and his buddy proudly showed their $30 prize for which Rick had paid $70. Through the alcoholic haze Rick came to realize that to take the clock home to Esther would be to heap more coals on her mounting discontent and impatience with the man he had become. So he gave the clock to the barmaid and staggered home $70 poorer.

Esther tried her very best to help Rick pull himself together. While he inflicted no physical harm upon her, he had been increasingly neglectful and undependable. Perhaps some defensive mechanism within him moved Rick to make false accusations against her. Although Esther was completely blameless, Rick's inner realization that his sexual prowess was succumbing to the steady alcoholic diet may have led him to charges against Esther ranging from frigidity to outright unfaithfulness. Night-long arguments ensued. One morning after a particularly disgraceful night of unfounded charges by Rick, Esther delivered an ultimatum: Straighten up or get out.

Brought up short by the realization that he was on the verge of losing perhaps the last friend he had, Rick stayed home from work and pondered the possibility. To help him think he ordered up an extra bottle. By nightfall he was in another of his alcoholic stupors. The arguments broke out again. He passed out. The next morning he awoke to find Esther packing her belongings. Panic stricken, he begged her forgiveness; promised her to stop drinking and restore himself to the kind of man he had once been.

Rick's intentions were of the very best. Somehow or other he managed to make it through that day without a drink. After a shaking and sleepless night he made his way unsteadily back to his office with another of his endless excuses that he had been ill. But this time there was no mistake. The boss was not buying; he was not giving any more chances. He was through with Rick. But there was one thing the boss had not reckoned with. It had been with great ingenuity that Rick had been able to obtain his liquor even when the bars and stores were closed and even when he had no money. After their savings had disappeared and bank loans had to be floated from time to time to support Rick's extravagance born of his drinking, great powers of persuasion had to be brought to bear in order to secure extensions on those loans when there was no money on due dates. It had taken great intellect for Rick to rise to the heights from which he was now about to tumble. In one last desperate plea, he called on all that ingenuity, persuasiveness and intellect to move the boss to demote him and give him a chance to work his way back up. So, he was not yet unemployed.

In the days that immediately followed there was a great deal of personal re-examination on Rick's part. His pride had been deeply wounded; it took all the courage he could muster to face his associates at work as he went about his subordinate duties in a job he had risen above five years earlier. The cut in pay had further strained a budget that was already too tight. One by one all of his old friends had dropped him. And his truce with Esther, Rick realized, was extremely delicate. He went through the motions of trying to behave himself. But there was always a bottle hidden somewhere in the apartment for his solace when the craving for a drink became too great. When he went out for a haircut on Saturday Esther knew that it would be anywhere from three hours to three days before she saw him again. He ate almost nothing, no matter how hard she tried to entice him with his favorite dishes. For his birthday she baked a cake and prepared a little private celebration for him when he got home from work. But he never got home until daylight the next day. Sensitive person that she was, Esther was never able to cope with the almost daily calls from Rick's creditors. It took all the strength and determination Rick had to satisfy the minimum requirements for holding on to his job, which he had come more and more to hate. There was nothing left in him for Esther. Not even hope. So now she, too, was gone.

Some weeks after Esther left Rick called the chaplain and asked if he would stop by to see him, saying that he had something he wanted to talk with him about, although the chaplain hadn't seen him in several years. For some reason he asked the chaplain to come by his place of employment, even though it was now about 8:30 in the evening.

The night watchman admitted the chaplain and directed him to Rick's department. The chaplain was apalled at what he saw. The once sartorially perfect Rick was a study in 'then and now'. His shirt had been worn for several days and the collar was frayed; his suit was badly wrinkled; he hadn't shaved that day but the scrapes from a rough shave the day before were quite apparent, and he was at least two weeks past due for a visit to the barber shop. He sat at a small littered desk around which there was the unmistakable aroma of cheap alcohol. There was a note of defiance in his voice as he said, "These bastards here are about to kick me out after I've given them all these years of the best anybody in my field has to offer. They don't appreciate a good man; they've got it in for me for some reason. I even come back, or stay here in the evenings to do the work of three men while they don't even pay me enough for one."

After a moment the chaplain asked him if he knew any reason why his associates would 'have it in for him'.

"I don't know the real reason," he replied, "unless somebody is scared I'm going to get along too fast. The only excuse they ever give is that I drink too much. But I recognize that for the sham it is. It is getting so I'm afraid to turn my back to anybody around here because if I do they will stab me in the back."

For about ten minutes he went on in this kind of shapeless accusations against his employers, his associates and a few other people he imagined had done him wrong and for no reason. Then he stopped and moved over to a file cabinet, the bottom drawer of which he opened. After rummaging around for a moment he produced a pint bottle from which he removed the seal. The chaplain watched as he tossed the seal to a waste basket and saw therein an empty pint bottle identical to the one he was now opening.

"Come on and let's have a little drink," he said. "It's been a long day and I need one to settle my nerves." When the invitation wasn't accepted he took a long gulp straight from the bottle and then set it on his desk.

"Rick, what has happened to you?"

"What do you mean, what's happened to me?"

"Come on, Rick," the chaplain replied. "I worked here with you for three years. We've been close friends and have been through enough ups and downs for me to know what you're thinking and feeling. I haven't seen you in a couple of years, but I still know when you are trying to pull a fast one."

He sat quietly for a while, gazing everywhere except straight at the chaplain. He moved again to the bottle and then said, "I guess you, too, think I drink too much."

"There is obviously something wrong. From your appearance, and the fact that you are headed downhill at a time when you should be moving upward in this company and your apparent need for the contents of that bottle and the one already in the waste basket, I would guess that there is a pretty good chance that you do, indeed, drink too much. What do you think?"

"Naw," he replied without conviction. "I just have a couple after work to relax me. A few on week-ends since Esther left me because there isn't anything else to do. But I can quit anytime. It doesn't mean anything to me."

There was another long pause. "Didn't you use to go to these A. A. meetings with that lush that used to work here? What was his name, — Jack something or other."

"Yes, Jack Stanford. Went off the deep end after his son was drowned. We went to the same church and were officers in the Men's Club one year. I'm certain he wouldn't mind my telling you that he called me once, as a fellow church member, to ask if I knew how he could get in touch with Alcoholics Anonymous. I found out for him and went to a few meetings with him."

"What kind of magic do they have, anyway?" Rick asked. "Old Jack was really on the skids. They were about to bounce him out of here on his ear. But all at once he straightened up. It wasn't long before the Pearson Company came along and offered him a helluva lot more money than he could make here. The last time I saw him he didn't look like he ever had a drink in his life. Driving a big Cadillac and dressed like a million dollars. That A. A. must really have something. Maybe I'll look in on them some time."

"Rick," the chaplain said, "I know a few of the leaders in A. A. I'll be glad to call one of them and have him take you to a meeting."

"Oh, no," he said. "If they really wanted me, somebody from the outfit would invite me. I don't want to go somewhere I'm not wanted."

The chaplain told that as far as he knew, A. A. members seldom if ever actually invite anybody in. But, they go out of their way to make it known that their services and fellowship are available to anybody, regardless of race, religion, creed or station in life. They welcome calls from complete strangers who need their fellowship.

"Well, what do I have to do to go in and look them over?" he asked.

The chaplain told him that there is a meeting of Alcoholics Anonymous nearly every night in the week somewhere in the city and its suburbs. Branches of A. A. are listed in the telephone book and the chaplain suggested that he call and get a schedule so he could choose the time and place he would like to attend a meeting. The chaplain explained to him that he would go with him on the next night but that on the following day – a Friday – the chaplain was going away with his family for a long week-end. The chaplain again offered to call some of his friends in A. A. and have them pick him up and take him to a meeting. But he said he wouldn't do this; that he would make it in himself.

After urging him to follow through on the A. A. meeting and promising to get in touch with him when he returned the next week, the chaplain took his leave.

When Rick was called the following Tuesday night his incoherence suggested that he had been deeply involved with the bottle. As nearly as could be determined, he had made no effort to contact A. A.

The next day an effort was made to reach Rick during working hours. When finally he was gotten on the phone he suggested that the chaplain again stop by the office that night.

He still had not had his hair cut. His shirt was different, but it too, was dirty and worn. In general, Rick's appearance had further deteriorated. He had had quite a bit to drink and he accusingly spoke of "other people messing in my business," as if to suggest that the chaplain was intruding, univited, into his affairs.

The chaplain had learned from his visits to A. A. meetings and from many long talks with non-practicing alcoholics who had been helped by A. A. that nothing can be accomplished by trying to persuade a person who doesn't want to stop drinking. So the chaplain's visits with Rick in the next few days were limited to telephone calls in which he tried to leave the message that he was available to help Rick if he could at any time he wanted him.

Some days later, on a Sunday night in the middle days of spring, the chaplain's phone rang. It was Rick. "I am ready now," he said. "I'll do anything you want me to do." When it was ascertained that he was at home he was told to stay right there until the chaplain could get there – about 30 minutes or so.

"Come in; the door's open," Rick responded to the knock. It was a shock when the chaplain stepped into the apartment. Rick sat by a table in the center of the room staring at a brown whiskey bottle that had only a small amount of liquid in the bottom of it. As he crossed the room the chaplain noticed through the open door that the bed was in such a state of disarray as to suggest that the linens had not been changed in many, many days and perhaps weeks. Dirty clothing was scattered everywhere.

"I'll do anything you want me to do." said Rick, repeating what he had said on the telephone.

"Rick," replied the chaplain, "there really isn't anything *I* want *you* to do. But I will help you to do anything you want to do, so long as it doesn't include continuing your effort to drink the city dry."

"Well, I want to get sober and then stay sober," he replied.

Since he was shaking and looking even gaunter than when he had been seen a week and a half earlier, he was asked if he wanted the few remaining drops of whiskey in the bottle.

"No," he replied. "That is the stuff that got me in this fix. I can't see how drinking that tablespoonful can help me get out of the mess I'm in."

He asked about going to an A. A. meeting then – that very moment. He was reminded that it was now 9:30 and all the meetings would be over. He thought for a minute and said, "Is it

9:30 in the morning or in the evening?"

Rick was in that condition experienced by so many alcoholics. His system was somewhere near 100 proof from his whiskey intake. Although his capacity to walk and otherwise move was practically non-existent, it was not from the whiskey he had drunk that day or during that week-end. His condition at that moment was the product of many months and years of heavy drinking, improper eating or not eating at all; he was in a state of near paralysis, not so much from drinking in the last 24 hours but from the total of all his alcoholic intake in the preceding seven or eight years. By his own admission, Rick was at this moment in a state of moral, spiritual, physical and financial bankruptcy. His wife had left him; his friends had been alienated; he had 73 cents to his name; he didn't even have a clean shirt; on the table in front of him was a notice from the landlord asking him to vacate the apartment three days hence unless the rent was paid in full and one month in advance. He didn't know whether he had a job or not, but the evidence pointed to the probability that if he appeared on the following day he would be given his dismissal.

The immediate problem was what to do with Rick. He couldn't be left there alone. The chaplain was not the most squeamish person in the world but he had no desire to stay in that cluttered apartment with him. The chaplain could have offered to take him home with him, but he realized that there was a serious question as to whether he could make it through the night without experiencing delirium tremens. Rick needed nourishment but he had volunteered the information that he believed it impossible to eat a bite; that the sight of food would probably make him violently ill.

In their town there is a nursing home that specializes in the care of alcoholics. But it was reported to be usually filled to capacity and its rates were very expensive. But something had to be done for Rick and this seemed to be the only chance. The chaplain called the nursing home and found that they did have one of their rare vacancies right at that moment. Although the chaplain could not afford it and Rick had no money, the room was reserved for Rick's arrival within the hour, and the payment was guaranteed.

As they left the apartment Rick was asked again if he wanted the therapy of that last small drink in the bottle.
"No," he said; "let's go."

When they reached the nursing home the chaplain wrote a check for a week's care, using his following month's mortgage money in so doing. Rick was taken upstairs and given a pair of pajamas and a robe which, they were told, would be the extent of his clothing for the ensuing five days. They asked for the small bag the chaplain was carrying, containing Rick's toilet articles. His shaving lotion and hair tonic were removed, and the remainder of the articles put away for his use when he was up to it. It was explained that individuals in an alcoholic stupor will drink anything – hair tonic, shaving lotion, anything with a trace of alcohol in it. Rick was offered a drink of a special concoction having much the same effect as alcohol before being given an intravenous feeding. Once again he refused. He was led away for this and to be put to bed. The chaplain departed, promising to return the following evening.

After dinner on Monday the chaplain drove over to the nursing home. Rick met him at the top of the stairs. He was pitiful. Although the robe and pajamas furnished him by the institution were clean, they fit him poorly. He was shaking rather badly and his eyes were bloodshot. In his day of enforced abstinence there had been hours of bitter realization as to this station at which he had arrived. It is often said that the troubles of an alcoholic are magnified during those hours in which they begin to emerge from a bout with the bottle. If Rick's problems were magnified, he certainly did not underestimate them. He was deeply penitent for his conduct in the preceding few years. There was near panic in his manner as he acknowledged as if for the first time, that he had lost Esther and he spoke over and over of his hope that, if he could straighten up and lick alcohol, she might come back to him. There was great concern over the cost of the treatment he was undergoing and he felt certain that his job would be gone this time.

At this nursing home – it being primarily a "drying out" place to which heavy drinkers can come and sober up – various groups from Alcoholics Anonymous conduct guest meetings nearly every evening in the week. Attendance by the patients is not compulsory but the management encourage it. It was suggested to Rick that he attend the session on that evening. His reluctance in agreeing was obvious. The chaplain was aware of the great physical discomfort he would experience in sitting still for the hour. (One hour is the self-imposed absolute maximum length of an A. A. meeting.)

There were three speakers on the program. The first was a man in his middle forties who told of how he had left his poverty stricken farm home some years before to try to find a better life in the city. He found instead an overwhelming compulsion to drink, get drunk and stay drunk until he was eventually arrested and put in jail to sober up. After more than 200 arrests for drunkenness, for which he had served a total of more than eight years on the prison farm, he was exposed to an A. A. meeting under a program instituted by prison officials as a weekly opportunity for habitual drunks to learn what was happening to them and what could be done about it. He said that, after attending every possible A. A. meeting during that term of imprisonment, he had become convinced that he was the victim of an illness that could be conquered only if he never again touched alcohol in any form. "Forever is a long, long time," he said. But Alcoholics Anonymous does not suggest to its adherents that they resolve – silently or orally – that they will 'never have another drink'. Instead, A. A. suggests that the person with a drinking problem approach that problem just one day at a time. They are told that if they promise themselves each morning "I will not have a drink in the next 24 hours," – then the problem is reduced to manageable proportions. This man concluded by saying, "Hell, I can stand on my head for 24 hours. You know damn well I can go without a drink that long. Other people might tell you they have come into A. A. and stayed sober for a year or two years or five years. I ain't gonna lie to you; I haven't been sober but 24 hours. But there has now been 583 of them 24 hours since I took a drink. I ain't got much of a job; I drive a garbage truck for the city. But today I was the soberest garbage truck driver anywhere. And before I go to bed tonight I'll fall to my knees and thank my God because I am a garbage truck driver and I'm sober."

The second speaker was one hard to forget. She was a girl that looked as if she hadn't yet seen her 30th birthday. She, too, had come from a poor family from which she had tried to escape by coming some years earlier to the city. Being a new and rather pretty face in the neighborhood to which she went to live there was no shortage of invitations from the young blades. The trouble was that every invitation she accepted ultimately included a visit to the neighborhood beer joint. She had the first drink of her young life in one of these joints and she got drunk on this very first excursion into alcohol's never, never land. She found that she liked the experience very much. In spite of some rough mornings after, she pursued a social life that centered around a bottle. But as time went on she drank more and more and from the experience she suffered in terms of growing carelessness in her dress, cosmetic appearance and manners. It didn't take long for the invitations to stop coming. But her craving for liquor went right on. Having no training for anything else she had taken a job as a waitress when she first came to town. But pay from that job couldn't nearly support her room and board costs as well as the expense of an ever growing appetite for liquor. Besides, her morning after sufferings had made her less and less dependable to her employer. Eventually she was fired. Seeking a new job at the only thing she knew, she decided to combine the sale of her serving skill with an opportunity to keep in close proximity with her new love: liquor. So she found a job in a restaurant that also served drinks. The result was inevitable and swift to develop. Within two weeks she was fired. There was then a succession of meaningless jobs, each of which served to provide her with the barest necessities but a little money for her liquor craving. To supplement this meager income, upon which there were great demands, she resorted to selling her body. But there isn't much market for the world's oldest profession if the purveyor is half drunk or more, dirty and increasingly unattractive. On a desperate morning when she badly needed a drink and had no money she attempted to rob a small ice cream store with a toy gun. She was caught and sent to prison. There she, too, heard about A. A. She had great difficulty in concentrating on the speakers she heard; there was even greater difficulty in relating her own problems to those of the speakers, who so frankly discussed their own drinking experiences and behavior that was the product of those experiences. Then one night near the end of her 18 month prison term a girl appeared who told a story almost identical to the experience of this small town girl in prison dress.

Concluding her talk at this A. A. meeting at which Rick was getting his first exposure to the organization, this girl said: "It took me a little longer to find that it is true. But in A. A. nobody is ever alone. Sooner or later somebody will come along and relate experiences just like your own. If you will just keep your heart and mind open and try to absorb something of what you hear, you will – subconsciously, if no other way find out that everybody you meet has had a little bit of your trouble. Then one day, just like I did, somebody will come along who has been right down the same back streets and horrible alleys that you, the alcoholic, have travelled. That person will understand. If you will open your heart to what A. A. can do for you, you will come to understand what a terrible thing the life of an alcoholic can be if that alcoholic continues to drink. And you will come to understand that the alcoholic can be helped; all he has to do is turn his life and his will over to a higher power. That higher power can take over the driver's seat and steer you to the greatest satisfaction anybody ever knew. I am convinced there is no form of personal satisfaction better than that which an alcoholic experiences when he stops drinking and tries to live like a human being. I call my higher power "God". But you can call yours anything you want to, just as long as you acknowledge that you, yourself, are incapable of running your own life and that somewhere there is a source of help far greater than any you can generate for yourself."

As the final speaker came to the platform Rick was about to jump out of his skin. But there were two or three other new patients in the room equally as uncomfortable. Then the speaker began to talk.

"There are no requirements for affiliating with A. A.; no qualifications needed except your own acknowledgement that you have an alcoholic problem and that you are no longer capable of handling your own life without help. When I first come to A. A. I was asked how I qualified. I said hell, if gettin' arrested 243 times in 39 states and four foreign countries for being drunk would do, then I guess I qualify.

"Of course," he said, "getting arrested for being drunk ain't always a qualification. Out in our group there is several members that hadn't ever been arrested for bein' drunk or for anything else."

He went on to tell of his experiences as a cross country truck driver, a merchant seaman, a circus roustabout. He told of what a necessary part of his daily existence liquor had become. If liquor was not available or if there was no money for liquor, then he and his associates with the same problem would drink bay rum, industrial alcohol — anything that would lift from them the veil of reality. But he had been in this town for seven years and sober for 6 1/2 of these years. He had gone to work in a foundry as a laborer and worked his way up to foreman. To the extent of his ability to do so without actually harming another human being he had sought out every person on whom he had ever inflicted a wrong and asked forgiveness. Some of these people reacted harshly, but at least this man had made an effort to atone for his wrongdoing. Now he was sober and happy. The long years of physical abuse had taken their toll; he wasn't as healthy as he had once been. He concluded by saying, "I might not feel good when I wake up tomorrow morning. But I'll wake up sober and to me, who has woke up in so many dives and jails drunk, there ain't no greater blessin'."

After the meeting, as is ordinarily the custom, there was coffee and a chance for the speakers and members of the audience to visit. Rick drank his coffee very shakily but showed no inclination to talk to the speakers or the chaplain. Deciding he had had enough for one day, the chaplain went with him back to his dormitory and took his leave.

On the following night Rick was in a somewhat better condition. But he was still worried about his loss of Esther, his financial insolvency, his job prospects for when he got out. The chaplain promised him on the next day, he would find Esther and tell her where he was. He further promised to visit his boss and have a frank discussion with him about Rick's situation and try to ascertain his future job prospects. Then he asked Rick what he thought about the meeting the evening before.

He didn't seem to want to talk about it. But the chaplain persisted in his probing. Finally he said, "Well, those people have had a helluva time of it. But what has it got to do with me? I haven't got anything in common with them. I've never been arrested. I've never wound up in a jail. I don't see how they can help me. I'd just be wasting my time running around with a bunch of truck drivers, laborers, waitresses and drunks like that."

There was an obvious reply the chaplain could have made to this latter comment but he restrained himself; if Rick would just attend a few meetings of A. A. one of the speakers would surely give him that reply.

The evening's A. A. meeting was about to begin and the chaplain suggested they go in. Rick's reluctance was quite obvious. But he moved slowly toward the meeting room and the chaplain followed him.

The meeting on the previous evening had been sponsored by a group from one of the outlying industrial areas of the town. Its speakers had been representative of the working class. Tonight the meeting was sponsored by a group that held its meetings in one of the big churches in a better section of town.

The first speaker identified himself as an insurance broker. His appearance suggested that he had done well in his profession. Rick was therefore, a little shocked when, after identifying himself and acknowledging that he was an alcoholic and powerless to manage his life with no help beyond his own feeble devices, the broker said, "Twelve years ago tonight I was a resident of what passes as the Bowery in New Orleans. By whatever name it was called, it was skid row. A few years earlier I had graduated with honors at Tulane. From there I went into banking. Along with banking, my avocation was trying to drink New Orleans dry."

He went on to tell of how he had lost his job at the bank and then a succession of less and less meaningful jobs. He lost his wife, family, friends and finally his self respect. For some years he was a prisoner of the life that knew nothing other than the most menial tasks from which to earn enough money for a drink or two. When there were no jobs then there was panhandling or stealing or whatever was necessary to get a few nickels for just anything to drink containing alcohol. He described in intimate detail the vermin infested flophouses he had called home; how residents of such places even steal each other's ragged shoes and dirty clothing. He told of the doorways, hallways and gutters in which he had slept and characterized his life in those years as one great big gutter of hell with nothing at the end but death. On a raw, rainy night as he stumbled aimlessly along the street hoping to find a handout he came upon a lighted building in which there were voices and people. Needing to find warmth and hoping to find a place in which to hide for the night he entered the converted store building. A meeting of some kind was in progress. It appeared to be something like a church, but in his rum-sodden brain he perceived that it wasn't quite like church. There was no choir and no organ. There wasn't anybody he could identify as a preacher, and some of the people in the audience were smoking. There was a big board on the back wall with such words printed on it as "arrogance," "selfishness," "envy," "egoism," "jealousy." Then he heard the speaker saying something about these words representing 27 character defects, some or all of which are usually found in the person with an alcoholic problem. There were further references to alcoholics, alcoholism, and people who drink too much. This derelict was not capable of any great comprehension but as the hour wore on he heard somebody identify the session as a meeting of something called "Alcoholics Anonymous."

Suddenly the meeting ended and before an escape or concealment could take place somebody spotted the man who was now addressing the patients in this nursing home for alcoholics. On that night more than a decade earlier, some alcoholics who had conquered their problems and become self-respecting, self-supporting, non-drinking alcoholics invited into their fellowship the epitome of a slogan constantly before them: "There, but for the Grace of God, go I." The warm hand of friendship and help was extended this ragged, dirty, drunk stranger. Among them, these members of Alcoholics Anonymous found for this stranger in their midst the medical treatment he so very much needed, such food as he was able to eat on that night, and a place to stay. The next day they found clean clothes for him, more treatment, a little more food. And now, on this evening 12 years later, that drink-sodden derelict stood before Rick and several other shaking drunks trying to get sober. He was clean, well-dressed, obviously prosperous in his insurance business. And he was telling us "I know you have got problems. But my problems might have been worse than yours. By the Grace of God and with the help of a few of the hundred thousand non-practicing alcoholics in this country, I have risen up from the gutter of New Orleans's skid row to come here and tell you tonight that if you want to you can regain your sobriety and stay sober the rest of your life — one day at a time."

The impact on Rick — and on the chaplain — was something like seeing Jesus restore the blind man's sight, or cure the leper of his affliction.

The next speaker was equally impressive; he was one of the pastors of the big, socialite church in which this particular A. A. group held its meetings! He told of how his drinking career had been pursued in what he had thought was complete secrecy. He was unmarried and had fallen into the habit of keeping his living quarters well stocked with alcoholic beverages, from which he made liberal withdrawals during those periods when he was not likely to be called upon for his professional services. But this preoccupation had extended itself to the point he was grabbing a nip whenever he could, deceiving himself into the belief that chewing gum, mints, mouthwashes along with avoiding close personal contacts would prevent detection. But, like all incipient alcoholics, the scope of his drinking broadened to unmanageable proportions, eventual exposure and near-ruin. He had sought help from other ministers without success. It was only when he made what he considered at the time as a quite desperate step and went to Alcoholics Anonymous that he found true, effective help. Among others who had suffered the same problems, and who, in varying degrees had experienced similar need to conceal their drinking — it was among these people that he found effective, lasting help. This man of the cloth warned his audience that alcoholism is no respecter of persons, professions, class or creed. And he told them that not even in his complete dedication to God, nor among his associates in the ministry had he been able to find such comfort, understanding and meaningful help as had been so gladly extended to him by truck drivers, garbage collectors, taxi drivers, doctors, and all the other professions and callings represented in the membership of Alcoholics Anonymous.

To conclude the program, the speaker was a very attractive woman in her early forties who identified herself as the wife of a Navy Captain who had recently been promoted to Admiral. She had come from a wealthy family; had had all the educational and social advantages that money and travel could offer. In language and with a degree of sincerity that no printed word could capture she told of her own suffering and the pain and heartache she had brought her family with her uncontrollable, excessive drinking. "One does not have to be on skid row, in a hospital bed, or in jail to know all the pure hell of the uncontrollable urge to drink," she said. "An individual's realization that he is powerless over alcohol; that this helplessness has injured his family, his children, his friends; that his life and usefulness is slowly being poured out of a bottle — there probably is no greater misery on skid row or in hell itself."

Obviously an impression had been made on Rick. When he made no direct comment, the chaplain asked, "Rick, before the meeting you said that the speakers last night had nothing in common with you. Do you still feel that way?"

"Well," he said. "I guess this thing can hit just about anybody."

The next day the chaplain proceeded to do the things he had promised Rick. He had a little trouble finding Esther; she had got her divorce and resumed her maiden name, a fact that Rick had not revealed to the chaplain if he even knew it.

When the chaplain told her of Rick's condition, she was visibly shocked. With some hesitation she finally agreed to accompany the chaplain that evening to see him.

Then the chaplain went to see Rick's boss. Things were not so good here. Having worked with the chaplain a few years earlier, the executive felt he could talk freely.

"What's this preacher stuff in you that takes you out among the sinners," he asked the chaplain. "A few years ago you were wet nursing Jack Stanford. I guess it paid off because he straightened out and seems to be doing pretty good now. But this guy Rick; he's a real loser. You're wasting your time with him."

He went on to tell the chaplain how Rick's undependability, his failures had actually resulted in some serious situations for the company. On the last day he worked, for example, Rick had failed to verify receipt of a large shipment of supplies and the company had lost its discount on a substantial invoice. There had been other occasions when inordinate prompting had been necessary to get Rick to do the simple things expected of him. And then there was an encounter between Rick and an important customer with whom he had dealt before his demotion. Rick had apparently offended that customer with some drunken conversation. Another customer had lent Rick money that had never been repaid. The order was out to terminate Rick's employment.

From there he went to see Rick's landlord. After great prodding, he very reluctantly agreed to grant Rick a further 15 day extension for paying his rent, but the full arrearage would have to be paid at that time, he said.

The real bomb fell that night when Esther told Rick quite forthrightly that she had other plans for the future which could not possibly include him. It was simple to deduce that she was soon to marry another man.

On the final night before he was to be released the chaplain visited Rick again. He had, on his own volition, attended the A. A. meeting the night before. He invited the chaplain to attend the meeting with him that night.

There were three more good speakers, further indicating the cross-section of the populace that has found help in that organization. The real shock came when the third speaker mounted the platform. It was the old drinking buddy with whom Rick had visited the auction sale and bought the clock with $70 he so much needed for other things. And Rick said that he had once known two of the speakers on the preceding evening's program.

The next day Rick was released. He was still thin. But some color had returned to his cheeks and his hand was steady. His only physical complaint was that he was hungry. We went back to his apartment and tried to clean it up. He found a laundry-cleaning slip and from the chaplain's own meager finances redeemed a few clean shirts and a clean suit. Then they went to dinner.

After dinner Rick seemed disposed to talk so they took a walk, winding up on a bench in a nearby park. The chaplain knew there were many problems Rick would have to face immediately. The financial demands he knew to be confronting him seemed most pressing but the chaplain was not prepared to offer any suggestions. Then there was the job. He felt certain that the odds were against his getting another chance with the company he had served for so long. But these were not the things he wanted to discuss. He wanted to talk about his five days in a nursing home for alcoholics.

"In these last five days my entire life has been relived, just as I understand a drowning man sees his entire past just before going under for the last time," he said. "I haven't had my 32nd birthday yet. But already I've had a few years of marriage that were as happy as anybody ever could have. And I gave Esther a few years of misery as great as anybody ever experienced. With no more than average preparation and training I got a good foothold in a great company and knew the thrill of accomplishment and promotion. And now I know what is meant in the Bible about throwing pearls to the swine, because that's just what I did with my future there. Right this minute I know what it is to be on the absolute rock bottom. Sure, it must have been worse last Sunday night but I was practically embalmed then. Now I'm sober and I know that, physically, I'll be even better tomorrow.

"I haven't suffered as much as some of the speakers that talked — or would testified be a better word? — at the meetings I shook through this week. By the Grace of God I was never arrested; I never wound up in a mental institution, as I understand lots of problem drinkers do. As bad as my present circumstances, I heard men and women talk in the last five days of much worse conditions; lying in gutters, drinking smoke, (straight alcohol) bay rum, even witch hazel and hair tonic. I'm flat broke, but I've got a place to sleep tonight. I won't win any fashion awards, but my clothes are at least clean, thanks to you. It will take all the courage I've got, but I am reporting for work Monday morning, even though it will be for nothing but to pick up my pink slip and a little bit of money coming to me. But I would go anyway. One of the things several speakers harped on this week had to do with making amends with those people you've done wrong. I think the folks down at the company have bent over backwards to try to help me. But I let them down something awful. It probably won't mean anything to anybody there, but I'm at least going in and tell the boss 'I'm sorry'. And believe me, I am. But mourning over that loss, the loss of Esther, the loss of so very much I have let get away from me in the last year or two; these regrets, without some action to go along with them are not going to do me or anybody else any good. I guess I'm in hock to you up to my neck; I've never even asked how much it cost you to get me into the nursing home. You got my laundry out for me and I know you've spent other money on me that you, with a wife and growing children can't afford to throw away on a worthless drunk. So I'm not going to be a worthless drunk; with God's help and all the wonderful help that more than a thousand members of Alcoholics Anonymous right here in this town can give me, I'm going to try to rise above my present problems and those of the last several years.

"One of the things people kept telling me last week was that alcoholics are sick people. They tell me that some of the best medical authorities in the country now view alcoholism as a disease and its victims as sick people. They say that an alcoholic is a derelict, or a worthless bum only when, knowing he cannot handle liquor, he still won't stop drinking.

"Well, I am not going to claim I'm sick or have been sick. Maybe that's the way it was, but I'm not a doctor. I know that I was a worthless drunk. I guess I'm still a drunk, because I am convinced that I can never again safely take another drink. So I'll just be a drunk that doesn't drink. One of the speakers the other night got fired from his job as a bricklayer 20 years ago for staying drunk all the time. But he went into A. A., got sober and started on the way up. One good job led to another until he was assistant cashier of that big bank over on the west side. That was 13 years after he went in to A. A. Then he got to figuring that, after 13 years he had the liquor problem licked. He began sipping a little along. He did get by with it for a little while; about 6 weeks, I think he said, and then he went on the granddaddy of all benders. The bank took him back after that one and the next one. But six months after he decided he was bigger than the biggest problem he ever had, he was canned. Now he's a brick layer again. But he's a sober bricklayer and I never saw anybody that looked so happy. He said he might get fired again some time but that he never again was going to get fired for drinking because, one day at a time he expects to stay sober the rest of his life.

"One thing that disturbed me a little though, was the gloomy guys that got up there and told us that if we didn't stop drinking we were going to die. But I got around that one alright. I decided I was going to stop drinking – for the next 24 hours, anyway, and start to live."

The chaplain's own responsibilities and the demands of his job did not permit him to see Rick again for about ten days. He tried calling him, and he called the chaplain several times but they just kept missing connections. Finally, they did get together and Rick filled the chaplain in on what had happened in the interim.

As had been expected, the company released him. But what he had not expected was the immediate refund to Rick of the contributions that had been withheld from his salary in the past three or four years for the purpose of the jointly sponsored retirement program. This amounted to about $700, more than enough to settle his most pressing debts, including the back rent he owed, and to buy the bare necessities for putting on a better appearance while looking for a new job. In this respect, Rick was far more fortunate than many alcoholics when they first emerge into the new way of sober living.

In his second week of making the rounds of job possibilities, Rick answered an ad placed by a small new company in the same field as that of his former employer. When asked why he had left his last job there was a moment of panic with him. But he decided to tell the whole truth and frankly say that he had had too much trouble with liquor and had been discharged. But, he told his interviewer, he had met the problem head-on and was humbly trying to adjust to a life without his crutch for so many years — liquor. The interviewer, who happened to also be a partner in the company responded by saying, "Alright. We can't pay very much; the hours are long and the work will be hard. But if you will take a chance with us, we'll take a chance with you." Rick took the job, but at a salary even less than that paid by his demoted status at his old job.

They stayed in contact during the ensuing nine months. Rick moved from his apartment to another smaller, less expensive efficiency unit. He lived simply and worked long hard hours. In fact, about the only time he had away from the company was devoted to A. A. meetings and a visit to the chaplain about every ten days. But he was happy and he was sober. Stopping drinking did not end his problems; no reformed alcoholic ever experiences such a release. But in his new frame of mind, constantly aware that his life was dominated by a higher power, which Rick chose to call God, he faced those problems and either triumphed over them or learned to live with them.

Nine months after Rick got his new job the chaplain moved to a city half way across the country. For the first year or so they corresponded, but then they both became lax and the exchange of letters stopped.

The chaplain did not hear directly or indirectly from Rick until last week — seven years since he last saw him. The chaplain had been sent to a meeting a hundred miles from the old home town so he took a quick side trip to see some of his old friends, including Rick.

It had been a good gamble for both Rick and the small, struggling company that had taken a chance on a newly reformed practicing alcoholic nearly eight years earlier. When the chaplain called Rick his response was something to the effect that his visit must be an act of God. He was observing his anniversary of sobriety on that evening by conducting a meeting of Alcoholics Anonymous at the nursing home from which he had emerged just eight years earlier a scared, shaking, unemployed young man with a drinking problem. He told the chaplain he still had that drinking problem but he treated it by just not drinking — staying sober one day at a time. And he had much to stay sober for. He was now executive vice president of that little company. His salary was more than three times his highest earnings at the old company. He had remarried and was now expecting the arrival of his first child which, when it arrived, was named for the chaplain.

In the chaplain's travels he went to San Francisco some years ago and witnessed the incident of one of the old cable cars snapping loose from its underground source of mobility. The car plunged to the bottom of one of that city's steepest hills, turned over and injured several passengers, two quite seriously. As the chaplain watched the scene he heard another onlooker say, "What a terrible thing it is when one of these things loses its source of power." And he thought, "What a terrible thing it is for a hundred thousand or more good people to lose their source of power each year and become practicing, irresponsible, uncontrolled drinkers." But what a wonderful thing when one of these lost ones opens his heart for the re-entry of that Higher Power, with whose help the disease can be conquered, the old wounds healed and new vistas of life opened.

CHAPTER IV

"NOBODY GIVES A DAMN"

Man may dismiss compassion from his heart, but God never will.
— *Cowper*

Self-pity is the most destructive attitude in life.

Every step toward God kills a doubt. Every thought, word, and deed for Him carries you away from discouragement.
— *T. L. Cuyler*

Larry Jillson did not have the best position in the company but, considering his background and lack of formal training, he had a good and important job. Most of the time his performance record was as good or better than that of any other employee. It was that very performance record that nearly led to Larry's undoing. Although he had a prodigious capacity for work and all the necessary qualities for a position of leadership, he became a liability to the company. He established a reputation as the hardest man in the company to work with. Most of the time he was just unusually disagreeable; otherwise he was completely unbearable to those around him.

Larry went at his work with the same compulsiveness that marks a confirmed alcoholic's pursuit of liquor. His binge-like application to his work led to periodic states of complete exhaustion. But his exhaustion brought more than physical fatigue. Along with his weariness came deep melancholy, utter dejection and total inability to function in his assigned area of responsibility. He bitterly resented and resisted the efforts of his associates to help him and lift him over the rough spots. The depths of his depression could be measured by the extent of his stubbornness. It was inevitable that the day would come when the company would have to make a decision as to whether he remained on his job.

In one last effort to salvage Larry from the abyss of his bitterness the company Chaplain visited him. "Do you have anything that you would like to talk about?" he asked. "Is anything bothering you that I might be able to help you with? Just talking about things; putting your troubles into words sometimes brings inner peace and a new sense of direction. Please let me help you."

The hostility of Larry's reaction was indescribable.

"Who the hell do you think you are, butting into my affairs like this?" he demanded. "What do you care about me?"

"I care a great deal," replied the Chaplain with unbelievable calmness.

"Like hell you do," exploded Larry. "Nobody ever cared. My mother and daddy, whoever they were, didn't care. They got rid of me as fast as they could. I don't even remember them. They dumped me into a state children's home and never came back. I don't know what kind of blood flows through my veins. I don't know who my family was or where they are. I don't know who I am. You don't know who I am. You couldn't care about me. Nobody does unless they want something from me. I'm alone in this world; nobody was ever so alone."

The Chaplain waited quietly, sensing that the flood gates were opening and that more of Larry's hostilities would pour out. In a moment, with angrily flashing eyes, Larry spoke again.

"When I was 16 they kicked me out at the children's home and I was sent to a reformatory. That's where I got wise; learned the tricks of the trade. At the children's home there was this thing they called religion, a lot of this God stuff, a lot of protection. But at the reformatory I found out I had to fight for my existence. It was dog eat dog and you'd better believe I learned to eat them before they could eat me.

"I had a pretty good teacher. My best buddy was a real tough guy. He beat hell out of me every once in a while but he showed me the ropes and we stuck together. He ridiculed me and made me feel ashamed in front of the other guys. But a couple times when we were by ourselves he said I was O. K.

"When I got out of there I was old enough to get caught in the draft so I went in the Navy. What a bunch of suckers those guys were. I guess they found out some way or other from my records that I'd been in reform school so they all turned on me; officers, enlisted men, non-coms – everybody. I always got the dirtiest jobs. The only way I could get any liberty was by going AWOL. They had rules against everything I wanted or needed so I broke the rules. One of the petty officers got smart with me and I let him have it. It was just another fight for me but it landed me in a Naval prison. Somebody was always starting trouble and I had to finish it. They got together and gave me a bad conduct discharge.

"I just knocked around then, getting a job when I could and staying with it till everybody ganged up on me again and then I'd quit or get fired. Mostly I'd get fired. It's the same thing here; everybody's got it in for me and I'm gonna get booted out again. It'll be the same in the next place."

After a little pause he cocked his head with a curious expression and asked the Chaplain, "Just tell me something. How the hell would you feel if your old man and old lady had dumped you into an orphanage, run off and left you for somebody else to take care of, not even letting you know who you are? How would you feel having to take a lot of gaff from everybody you meet, always having somebody wanting to do you in? Wouldn't you want to fight back?"

Calmly, and looking straight into Larry's eyes, he answered, "I suppose if I had ever felt so much alone – if I had been through what you have, I might have responded as you have. Does that surprise you?"

"Well, — yes," he said. "Nobody ever told me before that I have a right to my feelings."

"Everybody has a right to his own feelings," the chaplain said. "This is what we are talking about now, how you feel."

"You mean you are not going to hand me a lot of 'God stuff', or preach me a sermon on what I need to be, or am supposed to do?"

"No," said the chaplain, "I am not going to preach you a sermon. I don't think you need one. I think you need to know that there is someone who is interested in you. I'm old enough to be your father; maybe you can talk to me as you would have liked to talk with your father many times."

"Hell!" Larry exploded again, "I don't even know what a father is. What do you mean that you are old enough to be my father or that I can talk to you like a father? I don't have any idea what talking to a father is like."

The chaplain waited calmly while Larry seemed to be assessing this conversation that was so strange to him. At length he said to the chaplain:

"I must be going soft in the head or something. All at once it seems like you *do* care something about me. I've always wanted to know what it's like to have a father to talk to; an old man to help me through the things I was facing. But what's your angle? Are you just trying to convert me? I think you just want to add another name to the list of people you say you have helped."

"No," said the chaplain, "I don't happen to have one of those lists. If you could believe that I am concerned about you and you are willing to leave it there, we will see where we can go from here."

The ice was broken with Larry. Several more conferences followed in which a little more progress was made in identifying and discussing his hostilities. Then the chaplain told him about how psychiatrists, psychologists and chaplains often work together in trying to meet the particular needs presented to them. He was told of one particular psychiatrist, Dr. Hugh Missildine, who had written a book called *Your Inner Child of the Past*, which details problems similar to Larry's strange, remote and, perhaps extreme, experience. This book shows how every adult is at times influenced by his 'inner child of the past' and how that situation must be dealt with. Each person, according to Dr. Millildine, must accept the fact that he cannot blame his parents or their lack of interest, or what happened to him in his childhood for his continuing to be as he is. He must accept the responsibility himself.

Dr. Missildine's ideas were further shared with Larry. First, this psychiatrist believes that people who have been rejected in their childhood tend to be easily hurt and become bitter and hostile. They are so certain they have been unwanted and nobody will ever want them that they see rebuff, or rejection in and are offended by what others might consider just ordinary conversation. These sensitive individuals are actually suspicious of any friendly overtures made to them. The deeply imbedded feelings of the inner child of the past are difficult to overcome. These people are quick to believe that anyone who is friendly is merely leading up to another hurtful rejection. These people test the sincerity of any friend who finds them attractive, interesting, and desirable company. They will behave in such a hostile or obnoxious way that they force most people to reject them or abandon efforts to be friendly.

When portions of this book were read and explained to Larry, his response was, "Well, I'll be dadblamed! You mean here is a man who has worked with people and found that anyone who's gone through my experiences would naturally act out in these ways? Do you mean I am not crazy — that under the same circumstances most anyone would have reacted in the same way?"

"Yes," the chaplain assured him. "It is a scientific fact that human nature will react in certain ways under certain conditions; that the only way a human being can refrain from reacting in these ways is to find a strength of God's that's higher than himself, come to an understanding of himself and begin to act as a parent to himself so he might channel his reactions in a different direction.

"Alcoholism is another sign of rejection in childhood. Under the influence of alcohol a man may be able to relent in his rejection of himself and enter into the jovial company of those around him. Without alcohol, the alcoholic is unable to accept any real depth of feeling. He is uncomfortable, anxious and distrusting in the midst of any friendliness and warmth."

It was explained to Larry that Dr. Missildine had noted that every rejected person has a built-in short-circuiting mechanism which destroys most of his opportunities for any kind of a stable and continuing relationship. Also, such a person tends to be deeply attracted to people who are unkind to them, who treat them with contempt or may even physically abuse them. The rejected person is almost totally blind to such attitudes. He is deeply hurt by this continued treatment, yet cannot easily withdraw from it. One word of affection from the unkind, cruel and abusive partner means everything to him. Larry's gratitude to his reformatory buddy is an example. In effect, what is often recreated in the close relationships of such individuals is the entire atmosphere of childhood in which the child felt that he had been rejected in some way. As these observations from the outstanding psychiatrist were pointed out, Larry was full of wonderment.

"Well, I declare. He is describing me over and over again in everything you have said. Now, I must admit that this is helpful. Before these conferences, I wouldn't have listened to you. But I have been miserable in my existence. The fact that you and I are friends has opened up the road of acceptance within me. I know you accept me as I am and you are willing to take me as I am. I don't mind telling you that it really helps!"

This was the beginning of a change in attitude and spirit of Larry Jillson. He began reading books on religion and sharing his feelings about religion. This enabled him to separate the reality of God from some of the institutionalized forms of religion and cliches that had caused much rebellion; the 'God stuff' of the children's home. As the hostility deceased, he began to listen more and be aware of God's presence. There came a willingness to believe and receive God into his life. One day in conference with the chaplain, he said, "I am ready to quit running my life and let God take it and make something out of it. What is next?"

"Larry, just tell God what you want to do. Pray to Him in the same way you would talk to a close friend."

"You mean like I talk to you?"

"Yes, the very same way."

"O.K."

"God, here I am a big mess. I have been a fool and I am tired of it. I believe You can help me and want to help me into Your way of life. I accept Jesus Christ as my saviour. Thank you, God. In Jesus' name I pray."

Since then Larry has completely changed through a personal relationship to God; his attitude now is wholesome and enables him to relate to people in a normal way. It is never easy, especially in such an extreme case as Larry's to make such an abrupt change, but it can be done.

Larry was asked to give a brief summary of how he found help and how he looked back upon his past life. Here is his own evaluation:

1. I realize that I was only thinking of myself and I was in no way concerned about what I could do for others. Now I know I was selfish. Three years ago, I would have said everybody else was selfish.

2. I saw that I was wallowing in self-pity. As I began to see into myself, I came to realize that self-pity is the most destructive thing that could happen to anyone. It was eating my insides out and I was my own worst enemy.

3. I was interpreting the world by what had happened to me. Every adverse opinion I had of another person, I learned was what I really thought of myself.

4. I reacted to the world in the same belligerent way I thought the world treated me. I was amazed as I began to practice what Jesus said about doing unto others as you would have them do unto you. At first, I thought this would be impossible, but it wasn't really hard. There was a deep, inner satisfaction when I was able to do this in relationship to one person. The harder it was to apply this principle, the greater the satisfaction. When I learned to love and trust one person, I was able to love and trust others. I found that love is the strongest force in the world.

5. I thought I knew what I wanted. Formerly I had wanted to get even with the world and spit in God's face for letting things happen to me as they did. I am glad that God did not give me what I thought I wanted but sent someone to understand and help me even when I didn't want to be helped.

I needed God's healing. His love. His forgiveness. I needed a friend, someone I could trust. Through God and through other people who began to be true friends to me, I have been freed from the bondage of the past.

6. I came to accept the fact that I can and should be responsible for what I am and what I do. Even though I had had some tough breaks, it was up to me as to what my life would be from now on. I liked being a parent to myself, once I could accept this far-out idea. So I began treating myself as I thought a parent should treat a child. In this way I guided myself through some of the emotional barriers that had been real stumbling blocks to me.

One day the chaplain said, remember: this can be the first day of the rest of your life. That got home to me. It seemed God was saying, "Larry, from now on everything about your life can be different. This can be the first day of that new life." That was the beginning of a new and different me.

7. I believe God wants to help me. I believe the chaplain wants to help me and these other people, who know God wants to stand by me. I am going to do my best to help others. "These past three years have not been easy, but I thank God I got started and I am not what I used to be."

Someone said a long time ago, yes, twenty centuries ago, that you shall know the truth and the truth shall make you free. This is a good, although extreme, example of one who came to know the truth about himself, about God, and now he is free.

CHAPTER V

"UPON REACHING THE GOLDEN AGE"

While one finds company in himself and his pursuits, he cannot feel old, no matter what his years may be.
— *A. B. Abott*

When a noble life has prepared old age, it is not decline that it reveals, but this first day of immortality.
— *Mad. de Stael*

The golden age is before us, not behind us.
— *St. Simon*

Jim Long had been with the company since he was a young man. And now the time had come for him to retire. Among those who knew him well, was no reason to believe anything except that Jim was just entering into another phase of a very happy life. He was closing out a career in which he had been very happy and productive; he had made hundreds of friends. He enjoyed good health; he seemed well adjusted emotionally, and he had a little house and garden. But after six months Jim dropped in to see the company's chaplain. It was the first he knew or even suspected that things were not right with Jim.

For 45 years Jim had taken great pride in his work. That pride was evident by the high quality of performance in the department over which Jim had supervision. He came early and stayed late to get the job done. He always had time for a kind word for the young men and women working under him. His method of training transferred to these younger people much of the fine quality that made Jim such a popular individual. During the work week he gave so much of himself to his job and to the company's interest he was glad for the week-ends and a chance to rest, go to church, work in his garden a little and visit with his family and neighbors.

When retirement came, the first few weeks seemed like just an extended week-end. But it wasn't long before he had completely caught up with his gardening and all the little chores at home. His neighbors had not yet reached retirement age so they were seldom around except on week-ends. Although he was a devoted, tithing church member, his connection in this respect had been limited to church attendance and willingness to give of his substance. His wife had grown accustomed during his 45 year career to having the house to herself during the day. It was almost inevitable that an unoccupied husband would be in her way. Jim knew he was under foot to her and this just added to his feeling of utter uselessness. He had become very lonely and disattached.

Jim dropped in at the company from time to time. But this just added to his depression. He was now on the outside looking in; it bothered him considerably to see somebody else occupying his old office; sitting at his old desk, carrying out his old responsibilities. Not that it bothered him to see somebody else getting along; he had personally trained the young fellow to take over for him when he retired. But it hurt to no longer be a member of the team and it was sad to Jim that his usefulness to the company had ended.

And then came his visit to the chaplain.

"If I had known retirement was going to be like this," he said,

"I wouldn't have wanted to live to retirement age. Never in all my life have I felt so completely worthless, useless — even unwanted."

It was then that the Chaplain realized what a terrible thing it is for a man to commit himself devotedly to his employment over a long period of time and then, upon reaching the golden years of retirement, be so totally unprepared for it as was Jim. God and nature prepare adults to venture into the unknown depths of leaving sheltered homes when they first start to school. If they will but accept His help, God gives them the resiliency with which to face the world when they first strike out to make their own livings in the individual professions or trades. He gives them the basic understandings with which to build the new experience of marriage on foundations that grow stronger with the passing of time. And God gives the strength to face the new demands upon them when they become parents; the courage to cope with many crises we all experience in adulthood. But in His wisdom, He leaves it up to each individual to make the adjustments necessary when working years are finished and at last they have time to relax and enjoy such fruits as productive lives have made possible.

Nobody so richly deserved the peace, rest and happiness of a good retirement as did Jim. He had been a faithful employee; he had earned the golden years that were now within his grasp but which were so painfully eluding him. Even in the past decade or two, when such great progress has been made in identifying the needs of mankind and supplying those needs, the welfare of those men and women who reach retirement age has been largely overlooked. Population-wise, the number of such people vastly increases each year. Better, safer working conditions and unbelievable progress in medical science have made this true. A much larger number of people each year need to be made wise in planning an important period of our lives which God left to us to develop for ourselves. The chaplain firmly resolved to commit much more of his own time and energies to helping retirees, as a class, to recognize their needs for retirement life and to help them make the necessary preparations. Meanwhile, and of pressing urgency, was the need to find some way to keep Jim — this very worthy and capable man — from deteriorating to a miserable, vegetable existence. His frustrations had already led him to the psychiatrist's couch; they could lead him to institutional life — even to death.

The first step was to visit the company President and lay Jim's case before him. The President came up with a fine solution for taking care of Jim's problem for an interim period during which counseling and other assistance would be made available to Jim for adjusting to his long range needs as a retired employee.

At the President's suggestion, and with his authority, the chaplain called Jim and asked him to come to his office at the earliest possible time. He came the next morning – bright and early.

"Jim," he said, "the company needs your help, and on a very special basis. The President has asked if you will come back for a few months in a consulting capacity. Your principal duties will be to review the personnel training program in your old department for the purpose of making an objective report on whether your methods are making an acceptable transformation under the management of your successor. You will have no authority to make changes; in regard to this assignment you will communicate only with the President. The proper channel of communication will be through him for his consideration in light of company policy. There is just one catch to this: we will have to ask you to come back without compensation. The year's budget has already been made up and there is no money in it to pay for this service. You have indicated that your retirement pay is more than adequate to meet your needs. And, in consideration of the service you will be rendering the company, you will be given your own office with such service as you will need from the secretarial pool. Your title will be "Special Assistant to the President", and you will make your own hours, set your own pace. But the boss hopes you will be able to complete this assignment within a few months."

The chaplain had never seen such joy as that which lighted Jim's face. As the President and he had predicted, just getting back in a limited kind of harness for a while was all the compensation Jim wanted. He reported for duty the next day. And the chaplain began his campaign immediately.

He encouraged Jim to drop by his office every day. He needed no further prodding. Little by little the chaplain opened the subject of the day when he would once again be a retiree. To prepare for this period, he suggested that Jim carefully examine his personal interests for the purpose of seeing what might appeal to him as a hobby. When he had selected something, the chaplain suggested that he visit the public library and get some books from which to read up on this hobby. The chaplain asked him to confide in him and promised that he, too, would try to get as much information for him as he could.

When they got past this one and Jim seemed to be earnestly looking into possible hobbies, the chaplain inquired as to the depths of his commitment to his church. He confirmed that through lean years and prosperous ones he had tithed and that he attended services every Sunday. But beyond his financial support and presence at services he had no further involvement. It was a very easy matter to point out to him that the satisfaction he derived from giving of his substance could not compare with the satisfaction he could get out of giving of himself to the cause of his church. He immediately agreed. Within a month Jim reported back that he had inquired into areas of church program where additional manpower was needed. He had volunteered to serve on the building committee and to oversee the day to day housekeeping program at the church. He also took on some of the missionary responsibilities and it was in this endeavor that he became completely engrossed.

The weeks hurried by and the day came when Jim reported his findings and recommendations to the President, asking to be relieved of his job now that the project had been completed.

Jim never did become deeply interested in woodcarving, furniture refinishing, or any of the other hobbies he had earlier considered. But he did become deeply immersed in the mission of his church and in every aspect of its program. He continued to tithe. But more importantly, he gave of himself to his church, his fellowmen and to his God.

Last week the chaplain had a visit from Jim. "Chaplain," he said, "my life had never taken on its full significance or meaning; until now I had never learned that when the heart is given to God, the hand is made stronger and surer for helping my fellow man."

The changing of the role in life is always difficult and especially when it has been over a great number of years.

For many men their work is the main incentive for their life to have meaning. Only as he finds a reality to what he is doing can a transition be made.

Too few realize that working has significance and fulfillment only as they help others to succeed.

THOUGHTS FOR CONSIDERATION

1. The strongest drive in man is for self-preservation. Closely related to this drive is the need to feel important and needed in a job, in the family, and in the circle of friends.

2. Retirement can make a man feel he is not needed and no longer has any value to others and in life.

3. Being able to move from one role in life to another and from one age level to another requires the belief that all places and ages are important.

4. Old age can be the greatest time of life.

5. Retirement can put on the positive look and reap the joys of a life wisely invested.

6. Too close an observation of work separate from life itself will be destructive.

7. God means for every stage and aspect of life to be meaningful. Man's part is to accept this meaning.

CHAPTER VI

"WHY DID DADDY KILL HIMSELF?"

You cannot prevent the birds of sorrow from flying over your head, but you can prevent them from building nests in your hair.
— *Chinese Proverb*

Earth has no sorrow that Heaven cannot heal.
— *Thomas Moore*

The Lord is my shepherd; I shall not want.
— *Psalm 23*

Yea, though I walk through the valley of the shadow of death, ... thou art with me.
— *Psalm 23*

Tim's father had been a fine worker at the plant. He knew his job and he did that job very, very well. He had the fullest respect of his fellow workers and the confidence of his superiors.

One of the great satisfactions an industrial Chaplain experiences is the friendships he establishes among the company's personnel. His first responsibility, of course, is to serve as a listening post for the troubled man or woman, to try to help develop for them channels of spiritual strength for guiding them through their dark days. But a huge collateral advantage is the friendships that spring up between Chaplain and worker. It was in the latter form that the chaplain came to know Tim's father. He, like most people, had his day-to-day problems. He worried through the childhood diseases and accidents of young Tim; he took seriously his obligation to provide as well as he possibly could for his family and for Tim's higher education. All in all, he appeared to be very well balanced. He had complimented the chaplain by inviting him to his home for dinner on several occasions and he had been impressed by the peace, happiness and contentment of the home and family. The chaplain had come to like this man. Therefore, the shock that came with the news that he had committed suicide brought with it a personal hurt and a sense of personal loss as well as an alertness to a need the family might have for him at this sad time.

Walking into a home at the time of death is always difficult. It is hard, even for one who has been trained to help grief-stricken families cope with their new problems. It is hard to find just the right things to say, to manifest just the right degree of desire to help. It is even more difficult in the case of sudden death and, perhaps, hardest of all when it is death by suicide.

"Why did my Daddy kill himself?" cried ten-year old Tim. "Why did he do it; why did he do it? I keep thinking I have had a bad dream but I don't wake up so it must be real. Why did my Daddy kill himself?"

"I can't tell you, Tim, why your Daddy did this. I never knew of any thing that troubled him enough for this. Everybody liked him; I liked him very much. He was my good friend. I share your loss. But I can't tell you why he did this."

"Do you think he just didn't love us anymore? I always thought he liked us. But maybe he didn't and this was just his way of going away and leaving us."

"No, Tim; I am sure your Daddy did love you."

"How do you know? Did he ever tell you he loved us?""

"Men like your Daddy don't have to tell me when they love

their families. I know just by talking with them. Without putting it in words, they tell me of their love for their families just by talking to me, — the way they talk about their wives, their girls, their boys. But sometimes things happen inside of people and we never know just what it is. Like in a machine — sometimes a gear breaks off without warning and the pieces go flying through and break everything else; just put the machine out of commission.

"But the main thing right now, Tim, is for you to just talk to me; talk yourself out about your Daddy. Tell me all about how you feel about his death. We don't know why he took his life. But if we talk about it enough we will find what we will have to do in order to live without him. Remember, Tim, this is the first day of the rest of your life. You must decide now what you want it to be like."

"We had such good times together," said Tim. "He would take me hunting, play ball with me, talk to me; we would go walking together. He was always so good to me. I can't understand this. It hurts so much. Some of the kids have already been over here and they asked me why Daddy killed himself. I don't know what to say."

"There is nothing you can say, Tim, except to just tell them you don't know."

"But it hurts so much. I can't keep from crying. Daddy always told me that nothing but babies and girls cry. But I can't help it."

"Well, your Daddy wasn't quite right about that. Boys and men don't usually cry as quickly as girls do. But you can't love somebody deeply without grieving if you lose them. And one of the things grief does to you is make you cry. This is one of the ways of getting some of the pressure out of you. You know, when a boiler builds up too much steam, you have to let some of the steam out or the boiler will burst. Men and boys are the same way. Grief builds up terrible pressures inside of us. The tears we shed let some of that pressure out. Another way of getting the pressure off from inside of you is by talking about the cause of that pressure. The cause for yours is great sadness over the death of your father. So you go ahead and cry. That will bring relief for the moment. But if you will talk to me about it that will bring relief for the days ahead and help in learning to live without your Daddy."

"Well, God let my Daddy die. I just can't understand that. They told us in Sunday School that God loves us and takes care of us. Daddy told me that, too. Why did God let this happen to us?

Doesn't He love us anymore?"

"Tim, there are some things God leaves up to us. God doesn't bring us sorrow and heartache intentionally. One of the ways in which God leaves it up to us to decide what kind of men we are going to be is by letting us decide whether great sorrow and disappointment are going to lick us or if we are going to be strong enough to rise above it. God gives us no burdens that are too big for us to carry. Sometimes people don't want to and just won't carry their burdens. But if we want to, we will find a way to live with our troubles and carry the burdens that are thrust upon us. I know because I wasn't but a year older than you are when I lost my Daddy."

"Maybe God didn't cause it all. But inside I can't help being mad at God for letting this happen. He could have just taken that gun away from Daddy. Is it alright to hate God?"

"God wants you to tell Him how you feel. But He wants you to trust Him, too. I can't tell you why God didn't make your Daddy put the gun down. But, you see, even though all things are possible with God, He doesn't always control every single thing we do. He gives us a choice. He gave your Daddy a choice. We will never know what was bothering your Daddy; we will never know, at the moment he pulled the trigger, why he thought it was the right thing to do. But God gave him a choice and he chose to pull the trigger. We don't know why he thought it was the right choice. This doesn't mean that God doesn't love you. It doesn't mean that your Daddy doesn't love you. Your Daddy showed you in many ways that he did, indeed, love you."

"That might be right. But I can't help feeling like God doesn't love me or He wouldn't hurt me like this. I can't help feeling like Daddy didn't really love me or he wouldn't have done this. Everything seems so dark and black. I feel so lonely. I've still got my mother but it is hard to think about not having a Daddy anymore; not having him to talk to, not getting to hunt and fish with him. I wish it could be yesterday again and I could keep my Daddy from doing what he did."

"Yes. There are many times in life when we wish we could turn the clock back and keep some things from happening. But that's something we can't ever do. So when bad things happen we just have to find a way to make the best of them. So you can start right now. You will have to be more of a man yourself now that your Daddy isn't here. And I want you to know that I want to help you every way I can. I knew him well and liked him very much. Life without him will be very empty, too. So let's help each other."

"Well, alright," Tim said. "It's going to be real hard. We had so much fun together."

"I know nobody could ever take the place of your Daddy. But I like a lot of the same things he liked and you like. Maybe I can do some of these things with you if you will let me. It would please me very much if you would look on me as kind of a second Daddy, or substitute Daddy."

The grief that Tim described is not unusual but it is, nevertheless, very hard to understand. It was not unnatural for him to blame God for the tragedy that came into his life. Talking back to God was really a form of prayer for Tim, and it is for others suffering a similar loss. He felt that both God and his father had rejected him. He felt that he had suddenly been kicked out into a cold, cruel world where there would be no more of his great happiness with his father. Emotionally, Tim did not feel that he belonged to anyone; did not feel at home or at peace.

People are complex in the workings of their minds. Children are the most complex of all people. It has been found that 90% of the people undergoing emotional problems had unresolved grief within them. Seventy five percent of the boys and girls brought into juvenile court have lost a parent. It can be assumed that among these unfortunate youngsters, the emotional log-jam might have been most severe if, like Tim, a parent had been lost in sudden, violent death.

It is good to be able to report that Tim managed to cope with his great problem. He was able to remember the love and respect that had existed between him and his father to the exclusion of bitterness and loss of direction in a life without that parent. Love of life, trust in God and gratitude for the brief years he had with his father have enabled Tim to achieve good emotional health and to be a leader in his school activities, church programs and a promising member of the community.

THOUGHTS FOR CONSIDERATION

1. Children form their patterns of emotional behavior by the time they are twelve years of age.

2. No child gets over his heartaches until he finds love and understanding.

3. In one study of children brought into juvenile court, 75% had unresolved grief as the basis for their wrongdoing.

4. Everyone has the impulse to fight back at that which he does not comprehend.

5. The deepest drive of self-preservation causes every individual to blame someone else for his failure, problems, sorrows, and disappointments.

6. The love of God can come only through individuals acting as the avenue for His love.

7. Grief is one of life's greatest heartaches. It requires the help of a trained person to guide the grief-stricken through their darkness and despair.

CHAPTER VII

"THE HELL YOU SAY!"

Life is fruitful in ratio to which it is laid out in noble action or patient perseverance.
— Liddon

I would so live as if I knew that I received my being only by the benefit of others.
— Seneca

Life will give you what you ask of her if only you ask long enough and plainly enough.
— E. Nesbit

The men and women who form the human part of a large company also, at the same time, comprise a small community not very different from a small town. Even in a small town the best informed person doesn't know every single resident, at least not on a personal, speaking basis. But usually there is enough exchange of superficial information that, when coupled with one's own observations and conscious or unconscious evaluation, the mental image of the lives of just about everybody in the community takes some kind of shape. To the man who is trained to keep "a watchful eye over the flock," the tendency to catalog individuals around him may be a little stronger. It was in his role as minister to the most personal problems and needs of the company family that the Chaplain became aware of Jack and his pattern of life as others around him observed it.

Jack seemed to have most of the assets that are usually considered desirable for a physically and emotionally healthy young man. He was moderately handsome, neat in appearance and appeared to be strong enough to take care of himself. He had a reasonably good job; a car adequate for a young man's transportation needs. There was no reason to suspect anything but that this was a young man who was enjoying his youth while waiting for the right person to come along with whom he would be willing to spend the rest of his life. He had a number of girl friends, but apparently no single courtship that went beyond two or three dates. In any given week he might be seen with three, four or five different girls.

The exact time that Jack met Mabel could not be pinpointed precisely. But looking back, a time can be fixed within a couple of weeks or a month. Because instead of a fairly rapid turnover in Jack's feminine companions there quickly developed a condition in which there was no turnover; just Jack and Mabel.

Because of Mabel the Chaplain had come to have a speaking-greeting acquaintance with Jack. But it wasn't the things the Chaplain knew Jack and Mabel to have in common that gave rise to his pondering of their courtship; it was a thing which he knew to be quite singular in their respective inclinations. Mabel was devoted to her church and its work; she had a part in all its activities. But Jack never accompanied her. In fact, in his visits among all the churches of the community on all kinds of occasions, the Chaplain could not recall ever seeing Jack in the House of God or sharing in the functions of any church.

Nevertheless, the Jack and Mabel courtship flourished over a period of many months. To the observers of the local scene it may have appeared to be the very happy preliminary to an ultimate betrothal. But the Chaplain saw a quality that may have been apparent to no other person. The bond that drew Jack and Mabel together seemed strong. But there was no visible evidence of any great happiness and satisfaction that should go with every courtship, particularly one so generally regarded as pointing to certain marriage. Missing were the relaxed attitudes and reflected senses of well being one expects to find around a happy couple. As the weeks passed the Chaplain thought he observed increased signs of strain; it seemed that the faces of both Jack and Mabel were developing lines of worry and concern. It was really no great surprise one morning to find Jack waiting when the Chaplain returned from an errand to his office.

Jack was obviously agitated. His eyes were red; he kept fidgeting with the zipper on his jacket. As is the unfortunate case with so many people, Jack had waited until the emotional dam within him had nearly burst before seeking the counsel of a trusted advisor.

He wanted to talk but he seemed to not quite know where to start or how. But it was clear that he had a problem he had to discuss with someone. In so many words he explained that his romance with Mabel had fallen upon hard times. After talking around the subject for a moment he suddenly turned and dived to the heart of the matter. "Mabel has decided it is all off with us. She says she doesn't want to see me again. She feels like this last year has all been a big waste of her time; she thinks I am just stringing her along."

Jack stopped talking and just looked bewildered. Finally, he said, "It's all just one great big ball of confusion. I don't know what has gone wrong. Things just started going downhill for no reason at all. I can't get her off my mind; it just doesn't seem like I can get along without her. I think she feels a lot the same way I do. But there just seems to be some great big difference between us that gets bigger all the time. We haven't been happy together for some time. But it seems like it is even worse when we are apart."

"Just how have you expressed your love for Mabel?" the Chaplain asked.

"Oh, in the usual ways. I take her places and buy her things. Oh, she knows I like her."

"Like her?" exclaimed the Chaplain. "I thought you were in love with her. I thought you wanted to marry her."

"Well, yes; I guess that's the way it is," Jack answered.

"What have you done about it? Surely you have told her how you feel and what your own hopes and desires are."

"I guess that's really the trouble. You see, I have never known anybody like Mabel. All the girls I have run around with have been different from her. I went out with them for another reason. When I got the one thing I wanted I got me another girl. I don't know anything about this love stuff. But it must be love because I just know I can't get along without her. And it's not because I haven't been able to treat her the same way I've always treated the girls. Maybe it's because she won't play like they always did that I feel this way about her. But she says I don't really love her because if I did, she says I would tell her I love her."

"Do you mean you have never even told her you love her?" asked the Chaplain.

"No. I've done everything I know how but I just can't say those words. I just wish we could wake up some morning and be married; together for the rest of our lives. Without having to tell her I love her and without asking her to marry me. That's just the trouble. She wants me to say some words I can't say. And because I can't say those things she calls the whole thing off. Maybe she doesn't feel the same way about me as I feel about her. If she did she wouldn't make such a fuss about just saying some words."

"I've never really known you very well," said the Chaplain. "I've seen you around ever since you came to work here but I've never known anything about you. Where did you come from? What did you do before you came here? Where are your parents? Have you got any brothers and sisters? Tell me about your life before you came here; tell me about your childhood."

"There isn't very much to tell. Besides, I don't know where to start. Anyway, what's that got to do with the trouble I've got now?"

"It could have everything to do with your problems of today. That's what we want to find out; your earlier life — the things you did then, the things that happened to you, your childhood — if we explore these a little bit maybe we can find out what it is that locks you out from one of the most normal of all emotions. Why don't you just start with when you were a kid, where you were born and grew up."

"Well, I guess there isn't too much to tell," said Jack. "I was born in the mountains of North Carolina, in a small town. Even though I was eight years old when he left, I never knew my Daddy very well. About all I remember was him being there some of the time. He never had anything to do with us. I liked him; he wasn't mean to us or anything like that. I remember thinking it was kinda special when he did stay home. But mostly he was off and going somewhere. When I was eight he just upped and left and didn't come back anymore. She didn't tell us at first but pretty soon my mother told us he had gone off with some other woman. She might as well tell us because all the other kids were telling us anyway about how our Daddy had run off with another woman and left his wife and five kids to root for themselves.

"My Mother had to go to work in a store to support us. When us kids were big enough we had to carry papers, do chores for the neighbors and about anything else we could find to do to get an extra dime to help pay expenses. And then we would have to make beds at home, and sweep floors and mop and wash dishes. We never got to see our Mother very much because when she was at home after work she always had to be cooking or sewing or doing something else us kids couldn't do. And she was always so tired she didn't talk much to us. When she did talk it was always about that woman my Daddy run off with. Man, she really hated her. When the kids got tired of cabbage and beans and hot dogs and wanted something else to eat she always said we couldn't have anything that cost any more because that woman took our Daddy away so we couldn't pay for anything better. When our clothes were ragged and patched and too little for us she said it was because of that woman. I never could have a bicycle because of that woman. We lived all cramped up in that little old house with a leaky roof and drafty walls because of that woman. I guess I just got to hating all women because I didn't figure they were any good for anything but busting up homes. I hated the girls, too, because they grew up to be women. As far as I was concerned there was just two kinds of women. The kind that took my Daddy off, making him desert his wife and five children; and the kind like my Mother, that was always too tired to pay any attention to anybody and not able to do anything but fix cabbage and beans for us to eat and sew another patch on the pants that were too little and faded. Man, I didn't like women for anything."

"But you did start associating with them after you left home," said the Chaplain. "You've had several girl friends around here before you met Mabel. How do you explain that?"

"Oh, you know how it is. Girls have a purpose. I used them for that purpose. But I wasn't going to let any of them get a rope on me."

"Do I understand correctly that your attraction to the opposite sex was solely for physical purposes, for purposes of sex?"

"Of course. What else is there? Except for Mabel, I mean. She's different."

"Have you never felt any sense of being attracted to a girl except for the sexual pleasure you might derive from the experience? I ask you these questions just so I might better understand what goes on in your mind. I'm not prying just to satisfy my own curiosity. If I know a little more about how you think, Jack, I will be better equipped to make some suggestions that might be helpful to you in your present problem. Just tell me about how you felt, what you thought about when you used to go out with other girls before you met Mabel."

Jack thought for a while. Then slowly and somewhat shyly he again began to speak. "I don't know all the nice polite words for saying those things, Chaplain. But to put it plainly, all I ever went out with any girl for was to get in her pants. I liked the act itself. But it seemed like I was doing something I needed to do just to get a girl to fall for me enough to let me have my way. And then I would just dump them. I didn't want anything else to do with them. If I could just get a girl's resistance worn down then I knew I was the master. There wasn't anything else I needed to prove. There wasn't anything else I needed to do because there was always another girl somewhere that would give me a new experience, another woman I could make give in to me."

"Did they all give in to you?"

"Well, not always. Sometimes they would kick and holler and maybe slap my face. I'd just dump them and go on to the next one."

"Did Mabel 'kick and holler? Did she slap your face?"

"Well, that's the funny thing. She wouldn't put up with any playing around. She let me know right fast there wouldn't be any advances with her. And the thing I don't understand about it at all is I didn't get mad. I just kept coming back and after the first time or two I didn't even try to make any time with her. Except for one thing, there weren't any arguments. Always before I didn't like girls for anything but getting what I wanted. When I got that I didn't like them any better. And if I didn't get it just hated and despised them."

"You said there were never any arguments except 'for the one thing'. What was that one thing?"

"Sunday dates. If I wanted her to go anywhere with me on a Sunday and it interfered with going to church or Sunday School or any kind of a church meeting she just wouldn't go with me. And she was always bugging me about going to church with her. I went once or twice just to please her. But if she really cared anything about me I think she would have gone with me when I wanted to go somewhere, or just to be with her. She would rather give up a whole day at the beach or in the mountains than to miss going to church."

"Let's go back for just a minute, Jack. In the year you and Mabel have been going together, have you ever compared your relationship — your friendship — with her to any of the conditions you knew as a child?"

Jack thought for a moment, then replied, "No. I don't guess I ever did. Mabel is just so different from anybody else I ever knew. There isn't anything about her that I could compare with my earlier life."

"How about the other girls you have known; those you have 'conquered'. In all of those experiences did you ever for a moment link them with any events you remember from your childhood?"

"Oh, heck yes. About all the time. Those that were pretty good and seemed to be falling for me; making a play for me, trying to get me to come back and sometimes hinting about settling down. When this happened it seemed like I about always saw that woman my daddy ran off with. The quiet kind that just gave, seemed to get tired of struggling and sometimes cried about it, I couldn't help thinking about my mother. The gals that liked it and wanted more and looked like they were trying to rope me in, I hated them for being forward and pushy. I figured that if I had already been married they would have tried to take me away from my wife. The ones that seemed like they were sorry afterwards and looked kind of sad and tired, in them I always saw my mother with her tired, beat look."

"Well, how about those girls you used to go with; did you ever tell them you loved them just to soften them up?"

"Hell, no!" he exploded, "I never told anybody in all my life I loved them because I never loved anybody unless this is love I feel for Mabel."

"Jack, in my opinion, it is love or you wouldn't even be here. Of course, you love her. You love her more than you love the way you used to use girls; you love her more than that vanity, or hate or revenge or whatever it was that led you to exert your mastery over them, make them submit to them. But the trouble, I believe, is that you have never before known love; you have never before been exposed to a situation in which mutual trust and respect were paramount factors.

"In your childhood it seems that your mother was so filled with her own bitterness and so preoccupied with her responsibilities for making a living for you and performing the domestic duties necessary in your house it probably never occurred to her that along with food, shelter and clothing, children need love as much as they need anything else. From what you say there was never any expression of love in your household. Love can be suppressed for a while but it cannot be permanently submerged by anything, not even by hate. We have talked a long time this morning. I'll stay with you and talk as long as you want to. But I think it might be well for both of us to take a breather now. I want you to go back to your job and think about all of the things you have told me this morning. I want to think them over, too. I especially want you to think about the experiences of your childhood and see how you relate them to your life here in the last couple of years. What feelings you had as a child, as compared with any similar circumstances or experiences you have had in the last two years here. Then I want you to come back tomorrow."

At the conference the next day Jack seemed little if any more enlightened than had been the case on the day before. He volunteered practically nothing to the session until the Chaplain asked, "Jack, did you know when your father left you for the other woman just what was involved in his elopement?"

"I just thought he went away with her because he liked her better than he liked us."

"When did you first come to understand the physical — the sex implications of your father's relationship with the other woman?"

"I guess it was when I got old enough to pay attention to the other kids talking about girls and the things you could do to have fun with them."

"Did you ever hear anybody talking about the sexual side of marriage?"

"No. The only understanding I ever had was that sex between a man and his wife took place only when they wanted to have a baby. When a married man was interested in sex for any other reason he had to find another woman. So I figured my old man was just a whole lot more interested in sex with that woman than he was in anything else."

After a little silence the Chaplain spoke again. "Jack," he said, "Do you think your father's other woman liked that sex, too?"

"I don't know. I reckon she did. That's why she took him away from us."

"That, then, explains your behavior with all the girl friends you had before you met Mabel. In the girls you were running around with you kept seeing that woman. In your successes with those girls, if they seemed to enjoy it, too, you attempted to punish that other woman by cruel treatment to these girls. You 'loved them and left them,' as the saying goes, because, like your father's other woman, they seemed to like it and you were just determined that they were not going to have this pleasure, not from you, anyway.

"Oftentimes there are circumstances in our early family lives that make it difficult to trust and understand people. Your sex education was acquired from the worst possible teachers, your schoolmates who knew little if any more than you. You grew up with complete misunderstanding and lack of comprehension as to the real meaning of sex in a happy marriage; you never had an opportunity to learn that, even though people sometimes find pre-marital sex and promiscuity enjoyable, it can be very damaging when the time comes to plan for marriage.

"You have been filled with hate for your father's other woman; contempt for the woman your mother became when she was abandoned and you have lacked understanding as to the real meaning of sexual relations between a man and a woman. All of these things have combined within you to build different kinds of resentments that have forced you to reject, in your mind at least, any of the perfectly normal consequences of falling in love with the right woman; the woman with whom Providence has meant that you spend the rest of your life. You have right within your own grasp a lifetime of wonderful happiness if only you will unlock your own heart. Your error has been in looking inward and looking backward to your own bitterness and to the unpleasantness of your own childhood when you should be looking outward and forward to the fact that the world can be right when you will let it be."

"The hell you say!" exclaimed Jack. After a long thoughtful pause he said, "I don't think I could explain any of this to anybody else, but I think I understand what you have been saying to me. What I don't understand is what will happen to me if I do what Mabel wants me to and say what she wants to hear and then she just makes a fool of me."

"Overcoming the hurtful aspects of love and your desire to be loved lies in your own understanding of yourself. It lies in your willingness to turn away from your own self-sufficiency and place your trust in someone who obviously merits that trust. If you will do these things, those painful emotions will just dissolve like so much smoke. You will discover that expression of your love in words is as natural as expressing your love for Mabel, as you say, by being good to her, buying her things and taking her places. The difference will be that you will have a completely new feeling; a warm happy feeling that so completely fills your heart there will be no room for fear, distrust and any thought that your loved one will ever 'make a fool of you'."

A few evenings later the Chaplain received a call at home. It was Jack, who asked if he and Mabel could come together to visit for a little while.

When they arrived the Chaplain took the initiative. He explained to Mabel the implications and influences of Jack's early life. It was not necessary to make any reference to Jack's affairs with other girls and why he treated them as he had. The emphasis was on why Jack had been unable to say to her the three most wonderful words in the world, "I love you." The inhibitive factors of Jack's contemplation of marriage were examined and the three of them treated all these emotions in a clinical fashion so that, with this visit and several ensuing conferences, it was clear that distrust, revenge, hate and lack of understanding had been driven from Jack's mind. Instead, there was complete confidence, mutuality of interest and radiantly happy countenances.

By his willingness to bring his troubles to an understanding third party Jack opened the door to a lifetime of happiness. A truly happy marriage has been the result. Not only that, the company got back a better worker than he had ever been before; a man who took seriously his own responsibilities to his wife, his company, his community and his God.

THOUGHTS FOR CONSIDERATION

1. Love is the greatest desire of the human heart.
2. Men have a tendency to use love to get sex.
3. Women use sex to get love.
4. Next to self-preservation the deepest drive is sex. This causes many of the emotional problems to appear in the sex relationship.
5. There are many enemies of love but none are more dangerous than hate and self-pity.
6. Love is a gift of God.
7. Love must be given before it can become a powerful force in our lives.

CHAPTER VIII

"I JUST GO IN CIRCLES"

Sex has become one of the most discussed subjects of modern times. The Victorians pretended it did not exist; the moderns pretend that nothing else exists.

— *Fulton J. Sheen*

For contemplation he, and valor formed; for softness she, and sweet attractive grace; he for God only, she for God in him.

— *Milton*

Love is love's reward.

— *Dryden*

Susan Moore was a lovely blonde. The picture magazines could have depicted nothing lovelier than her five-foot-two frame endowed with all the characteristics considered by her contemporaries as prerequisites for the beautiful girl. For the most part she had the personality to go with it all. She could be gay, witty, charming, and an all-round good companion. And she could spoil it all with her inevitable revelations of personal lethargy, aimlessness and a growing lack of personal values. On the redeeming side was her capacity to see what was happening to her, her ability to be genuinely concerned about the way her life was developing. In her favor was her willingness to seek outside help. She decided to take her problems to the company Chaplain and ask him what kind of professional help she needed.

In her first conference with the Chaplain she explained a childhood background that is so tragically common as not to warrant repetition here. Briefly, she was the child of parents who both worked. These parents were so occupied with their own problems, their own quest for personal satisfaction and overcome with the fatigues resulting from the pressures on so many modern working parents, they had little time for Susan. They saw that she was well dressed, that she ate regularly and had the necessary books, pencils, crayons and other equipment for attending school. Summertimes saw Susan shuffled off to her grandmother's home, which was really a source of joy for the child. There she could run and play and drink in the beauties and freshness of the wonderful rural scene, while being the object of her grandmother's adoring, pampering affections. None of these things — neither the indifference of life in her own home, nor the pampering of her grandmother — were possessed of influences that would lead to the wrong kind of life. But they were completely lacking in the training and formation of basic personal and spiritual characteristics that would help avoid the traps, roadblocks and tragedies that can come to a young person.

While she was unable to tell the Chaplain of any particularly unhappy experiences of her early childhood, Susan could not speak of any real personal accomplishments until after she reached high school. There her popularity grew as her physical beauty matured. She was elected as one of the cheer leaders and she became a majorette with the band. In her crowd there were kids who seemed to have no other thought in life but having a good time and maintaining a high degree of popularity, particularly with the boys. In time the familiarities reached the sex stage and going the limit.

Susan's grandmother died during her junior year in high school, eliminating that possibility for getting away, not only from her parents, whose failure to associate with their lovely daughter had put them completely out of communication with her, but also a chance to get away from her friends and reflect upon the effects and possible consequences of the social patterns she had fallen into.

When graduation came, Susan had no idea what kind of studies she would like to pursue in college; she had reached no decision as to where, or if she wanted to go on to school. So she found herself a job with this company. And now she was in the Chaplain's office, trying to find the way; trying to see if in some manner she could change, if not wipe away the manner in which she had come to live.

"Even in high school, sex seemed cheap, dirty and unrewarding. But it seemed a way of life that can't be avoided, no matter what the preachers and moralizers say about it. I am going with a boy now with whom I have been having sexual relations for about six months. After each time I feel like I have been dragged through the mud. It makes me feel so cheap. But he keeps telling me the same thing the others always told me, that if I really care about him I will go ahead. I don't want to lose him, like he says I will if I don't give in to him.

"All of our gang's parties are wild. We head for the beach. Everybody drinks, engages in sex, sometimes with different partners. Now we have added to our kicks by playing around with drugs. It has all got to be so meaningless to me. I don't want to live like this but if I don't I just won't have any friends; they will all drop me like a hot potato. I don't know what in the hell I am going to do."

"Well," said the Chaplain, "you might start thinking in terms of *what in heaven* you might do. It seems that you already have enough hell in your life. But it most certainly is not too late to let a little heaven come in. To get the help you seek, you must first sincerely and actively want it. Then you must get to understand yourself better, learn how to work with your emotions. And with your own personal sense of values, you might apply the same test you apply to spending your pay check. Ask yourself, before engaging in any of the pastimes that have come to be a part of your life, whether the price you pay in terms of self-degradation, remorse – that dirty feeling you say you have – are these things worth the acceptance you get from a crowd whose own morals leave so much to be desired? I think I know your answer. Coming here in search of help makes that answer self-evident. And believe me, I want to help you. Let us start by examining a little further into your thinking process. Tell me some more about your home life, your growing up and those years in high school when things apparently started going so wrong for you."

Susan poured out her heart to the Chaplain in this and in several more visits she made to him on succeeding days. Basically, it was just the story of a brighter-than-average, prettier-than-average daughter of parents whose combined earnings made for a higher-than-average family income. But in providing that income, jobs came first with the parents. They worked hard, drained themselves of all their energies during the days and spent their evenings in a terrible mixture of planning for spending those earnings, bickering over little things made important only by the nerves and tempers rubbed raw by the everyday demands upon them. In their own way they loved Susan. They recognized in her a brightness and self-sufficiency that made her unusually equal to the childhood demands of school, sub-teen age social life and the initiative for doing for herself those things that needed to be done for keeping her own little affairs in order. But what they overlooked was their obligation for providing substance to Susan's life. It had not seemed important to the parents to show their daughter any depth of affection. Susan never learned in her early years the importance of family, home, parent-child relations and parental guidance. Having no rudder, Susan's boat had to drift with the tide and the pressures of social winds among her school acquaintances.

Just getting these problems out on the table brought to Susan predictable relief. As she and the Chaplain explored her mental processes, answers began to emerge from the darkness that had descended upon her.

It was explained to Susan how emotional problems build themselves up, that there are these major involvements connected thereto.

First, there is the disorganized life, in which a person is unable to put his feet on any solid ground. Susan had never had anyone with whom she could relate in an important, meaningful way. Only as a person is able to touch with ideals of lasting value can a person touch with meaningful reality, find a base for life and place from which to embark upon living that life well. Susan came to understand that the shallow emotional base from which she operated had led to an aimless, disorganized kind of life for her. Her apathy, cynical attitude and lack of energy toward life in general were the consequences of the valueless answers that had been provided for her emotional needs. Indeed, she had had no basis for even determining what those needs really were.

Susan had followed a practice of acting out whatever came naturally to her, yielding to her impulses whatever they might have been. Sex had become a compulsive but unrewarding outlet for her; she and her boy friend were dumping unhealthy emotions on each other. Any relief from their frustrations was temporary at best. Recognizing this was to face up to the second major factor in her particular emotional roadblock.

The third was a condition often referred to by psychologists as somitization, the locking up of emotions within a person to such a point that real, identifiable physical infections develop in the body. Susan, by her inability to release her deep, underlying feelings, had fallen victim to such infections and was under the care of a medical doctor at the time she came to the Chaplain.

The alternative – or the relief from these conditions is to honestly pinpoint problems and find a way to talk them out with a knowledgeable, understanding person – preferably one who is trained in the science of helping people mediate their own conflicts. By coming to the Chaplain, Susan had done this.

Girls often use sex to gain love or acceptance. But the use of sex for these purposes can achieve no worthwhile benefit; can produce no sense of satisfaction except for a fleeting moment of physical sensation. This indictment does not apply solely to the male or to the female of the species. Oftentimes an unfair burden of blame is heaped on the male as the aggressor. But if there were no willingness on the part of the female partner the incidence of sexual promiscuity would be greatly reduced.

In Susan's case, she was using boys and letting them use her as each pursued the search for social acceptance and satisfaction for some vicarious desire to which had been attached, for lack of another definition, the term "love."

Through a series of conferences with the Chaplain, Susan was restored to a state of health in her emotions, in her sense of values and in spiritual recovery. These were the factors:

1. Susan came to recognize for the sham it was the part sex was playing in her life and the falseness of her reactions to her circumstances and environment.

2. A deep hatred for herself had developed within her which she

was letting enter into all her relationships with other people.

3. Susan was able to bring to the surface her subconscious realization that her excuses for immorality — "everybody's doing it" — were poor reasons for destroying her own inner resources, opportunities to live and chances for real happiness.

4. She redirected her interests and energies to embrace meaningful projects for the good of all society and, through involvement in the religious community, she came to a state of spiritual inner peace that manifests itself in the pursuit of eternal values.

THOUGHTS FOR CONSIDERATION

1. Time is of essence in having a good home life.

2. It takes a heap of living together to build a strong family.

3. Communication is an absolute necessity for love and understanding to be in the members of any household.

CHAPTER IX

"DEAR CHAPLAIN"

He who despairs wants love and faith, for faith, hope, and love are three torches which blend their light together, nor does the one shine without the other.
— Metastasio

Life is a warfare; and he who easily desponds deserts a double duty — he betrays the noblest property of man, which is dauntless resolution; and he rejects the providence of that all gracious Being who guides and rules the universe.
— Jane Porter

Dear Chaplain:

Maybe the return address on this letter won't surprise you too much. All the time you spent on trying to make me believe there was some good in me somewhere, you must have known there wasn't. The things I was able to do when you were counseling with me — they were not because I had any good in me, they were because I was smart. It was a case of a good brain but not much of a soul to go with it. But the return address is incomplete. After "State Prison" it ought to say "Death Row." I don't guess that makes any difference, though, because by the time you get this it will be too late for me to get any mail here. Just address it to me on the hottest street in hell.

I'll never forget the first time I ever saw you. I was some kind of messed up inside. That's the way I've always been. But I guess it was worse then than it has been most times except for when I got in the trouble that landed me here.

Anyway, I hadn't been with the company but a few months and I was already in Dutch. Just like all my life before then and most of it since I was at the end of one kind of rope or another. (That's truer than it might seem like because in a few hours I'll be at the end of my last rope, only it will be a gas chamber).

The first time I came to see you it was because I had got that little girl in a family way. Ordinarily that wouldn't have been too much of a problem. I would have just done what I always did before when things got hot for me, just take off. Only this time I couldn't. A month before that I tried to drink up all the beer in the Hot Spot over in town and then I tried to tear the place down and landed in jail.

When I came before the Judge he took a look at my record and found out I made a habit of that kind of thing. He found out I had already done time for using my fists to change people's appearances and changing the landscape in other towns over the state. But I guess he felt sorry for me. I hadn't been in town very long; and I had a good war record. The war hadn't been over long enough that that didn't count. Anyway he suspended my sentence and put me on probation. If I had broke that probation I would have had to serve a long hard year at straight time.

I had already begun to wonder what made me do the things I did; I couldn't understand why on pay day all I wanted to do was spend all my money on booze and raising hell. I couldn't understand why I couldn't use my brain and my energy to get ahead instead of just using them on some cheap job so I could get a cheap pay check to spend on cheap liquor. And then this girl comes and tells me she's carrying my child and her old man said if I didn't marry her he was going to beat me up and get a warrant against me for bastardy. Hell, I couldn't marry her if I want to; I already had a wife, even if I didn't know where she was. Just him trying to beat me up would have been the end of me. I don't know how to fight nice and quiet; any fight I ever get into half the town gets into before it's over. So you know the judge is going to find out about that and send me up to the state boarding house. And even if I was lucky enough to get by that one just having a warrant out against me would have put me right in the jail house. I don't know why I thought you could help but I was ready to try anything.

When I told you about it you asked me about all my other troubles with the law. In order to try to find out what makes me tick you asked me to tell you about when I was a kid. There sure wasn't much to tell but I remember how I told you about it and how much you had to keep urging me on to get me to tell you all about it:

I was born way back in the mountains in Southwest Virginia, near the Tennessee and Kentucky lines. My folks were awful poor but I didn't realize it then. Everybody around us was in about the same fix. I used to go with Pa in the wagon over to Big Stone Gap or to Gate City and then I would see cars and people wearing clothes so different from what we wore up home I thought they looked funny. There was a lot of stuff in the stores I didn't know what was. And when we walked by a hot dog stand I smelled food like I have never smelled before and it sure did smell good. But Pa wouldn't get me none; he just said when it came dinner time we would eat the stuff we had brought from home in a bucket.

I remember going to church with my folks. I guess that's where I got to where I didn't like church. We would go in and sit on the old rough benches and the preacher would get up and holler and shout till he couldn't talk anymore. Then some of the people would get up and talk about what sinners they were and they would holler and cry and fall down on the floor. They called it "testifying" and sometimes they got real wild and gibberish. I remember my Ma said they was talking in "unknown tongues." Church would just last for hours and hours it seemed like.

When I was about 9 years old we got a new preacher. He kept talking about "faith in the Lord" so much that nothing could bother us. To prove we had faith he had a service one hot summer night and he brought a box with some rattlesnakes in it. He asked for some volunteers and my Pa was one of them. I guess the only reason he did it was he wasn't just himself that night. Late that afternoon he and another fellow that lived near us went down in the woods to where they kept a still by a creek bank and they got a little high. Ma tried to stop him from going up there to the preacher and volunteering to show how much faith he had. But the preacher thought she was volunteering, too, and I guess she was too ashamed to say there in front of all those people that she was scared of those snakes. When they got the snakes out of the box my Ma and Pa and the preacher all got bit. Ma died that night. Pa lasted till the next afternoon. I never did know what happened to the preacher. He said he got bit and his faith healed him but I never did think he even got bit. Anyway, I was an orphan. Me and my little brother got handed around among the neighbors the rest of that summer and all that winter. As soon as the roads were passable the next spring they took us into town and handed us over to the welfare. The neighbors said they couldn't look after us anymore and I guess they couldn't because it was years later when I fully realized just how pitifully poor everybody up there in those mountains was. Well, the welfare didn't have anyplace to put us until they could get us in an orphange so they took us down to the jailhouse. The jailer, I remember, didn't like that much but there wasn't anything he could do but take us in. But he didn't lock the door. I didn't think much of all this so that night I slipped off and just started running. It didn't bother me none that I was leaving my little brother behind. I guess I knew by instinct that up in those mountains it was every man for himself if you wanted to stay alive. I didn't know where I was going. I'd never been anywhere except from our house back up in the mountains down to Big Stone Gap and to Gate City. When I couldn't run anymore I just got off the road and sat down next to an old log. I didn't mean to go to sleep but when I opened my eyes the sun was abut an hour high and I was facing it. I figured from that that I had been going west the night before and when I got up I knew I had to just keep on going that way.

    I realized I was awful hungry and the longer I walked the worse it got. After a while I came to a farm house. It was big and it had some paint on it. I decided I would try to slip in toward the barn and maybe the big old house, too, and see if there might be anything lying around that I could eat. I was scared to go up and ask for anything. I just knew they would take me back to the sheriff and I was afraid he might whip me. Sure enough, there was a bucket sitting out there and it was full of what looked like kitchen scraps so I just helped myself. I know now it was stuff just waiting for somebody to take it down to the hogs. But that morning it sure did taste good. After that I felt better so I started walking again. I didn't know where I was going or what I was going to do but I knew I had to just keep going. And the going was awful hard. Anybody that's never been up in those mountains can't realize how high they are or how steep. When I got tired I'd stop and rest. And when I heard a car coming I'd get off the road and out of sight until it passed. When night came I did what I had done the night before, just got off the road and found a log to lean on and went to sleep.

When I had been going a couple hours the next day I realized I was getting weak and knew I was awful hungry. So I started looking for another house where I might find something to eat. But the road here was almost straight up and there just wasn't any place in sight. I never saw anyone except in the cars that went creeping by as they crawled up the mountain.

When the sun was about straight overhead I came to a car that was stopped on the road. There wasn't any side of the road to pull off on. I wasn't scared to walk up to it because it was plain that it was a man and woman with four kids. I knew it wasn't the sheriff and my insides told me they were not looking for me. When I got up close I saw the man bending over the engine like he was fixing something. The woman and one of the kids had got back in the car and was getting something out of a basket. It turned out to be fried chicken. Just seeing them eat it I thought I was going to be sick to my stomach if I didn't get some, too. Suddenly the man straightened up and he saw me and called out, "Hey, boy – ." My first thought was to turn and run but I guess I was just too weak and maybe a little hypnotized by that food. But I took another step or two towards him and he said, "My old car got too hot climbing this mountain and the water boiled out. Do you know where I can get any?"

It was the first time I ever knew you put water in a car. But I did remember a ways back when I had jumped off the road when a car was coming I seen a spring running out of a mountain on the other side of the road. So I told him about it.

The man opened the car door and pulled out a bucket. He emptied some apples on the floor of the car and handed the bucket to me and said, "I'll give you a dime if you will go back down there and fill this up and bring it back to me."

I had heard about dimes and knew they were money but I didn't know how much money it was. But I did know about apples and fried chicken. So I told him I would rather have some of that. They were real nice about it and gave me a drumstick and a cold biscuit. I must have swallowed them down in one bite and they sure did taste good. Seeing how I gobbled it up the woman said, "You look like you could do with another piece." So I gobbled that up, too. Then the man handed me the bucket and I headed back for where I saw the water, hoping that when I got back with it they would give me some more chicken.

Sure enough they did, and an apple too. Then the man asked me where I was going. Since I didn't know I said, "Just up the road a piece." He said they were a little crowded up already but if I wasn't going far to hop in and they would give me a ride. It was the first time I had ever been inside a car, let alone ride in one.

We hadn't gone very far when I could tell from the way the man was grunting and mumbling to himself that something was wrong. Then I saw the steam rising up in a big cloud in front of the car. But on the curve up ahead there was a little store which the man said was a filling station. So we limped on in there. When he asked the man at the filling station to take care of his car for him he turned and asked how much farther I was going. Feeling like my luck might run out I looked out across the way and then answered, "Just across that there ridge." So he said, "I guess you might as well just go on then because it will take a while before the car cools off enough to put any water in it. "So I started walking and then he called me back. "Here's the dime I promised you," he said. I didn't know what to do with it so I took it and put it in my pocket and then I was on my way.

I kept on walking but I followed my practice of getting out of sight when I heard a car coming. After a while when I had to get off the road the car that passed was the one I had been riding in.

There was another night on the road, or just off the road. The next morning it was drizzling rain when I woke up. After I had been walking about 2 hours I saw another store up ahead, which I recognized this time as another filling station. Feeling hungry again, and remembering the dime I had, I walked into the filling station, where there was a show case full of stuff I didn't know what was, but it looked so good I figured it was something to eat. I asked the man how much of that stuff a dime would buy me and he handed me two cakes. They were real sweet and had something white and like real thick milk inside them and they sure did taste good. By then it was raining real hard and I didn't figure there was any harm in staying in here out of the wet. But it rained all day, hard most of the time. The man was nice, though, and didn't bother me none. He did ask me where I was from and when I told him he said, "That's a right far piece from here." When he asked if my ma and pa knew where I was I told them about the snakes and that I didn't have any ma and pa. Then he asked me where I was going to sleep that night. He had just told me I was a right far piece from where I had run away from the jail so I felt like I didn't need to be quite so careful now. I told him I didn't have any place to stay. So he said he lived in the back of the store and if I didn't mind sleeping on some old blankets on the floor I could stay with him. That was wonderful news. But the best thing was when it got dark and he closed up the store we went in the back where he had a kerosene stove and a couple of blankets as well as a cot he slept on. It turned out he didn't have a wife, just lived there by himself. He lit that stove and in a few minutes he brought out some country ham, which I thought was going to drive me crazy when I smelled it frying. He also made some biscuits and warmed over some greens and cooked some potatoes. Man, I still remember that as the best meal I ever had in all my life.

The next day the man, who told me to just call him "Matt", questioned me about who I was and where I had come from. I must have satisfied him because he finally said, "Well, there seems like there is just a little too much for me to do around here by myself, especially with summer coming on and the tourists in their cars, most of them boiling by the time they get this far up the mountain. If you want to stay around here and help me out for a while you'll be welcome. I can't pay you much, but I'll fix you a regular bed and you can sleep back there with me and we'll have something or other to eat every morning and every night."

Chaplain, I guess the next two years was the happiest of my whole life. Matt didn't talk much and he didn't ask much of me. True to his word, he couldn't pay me much. A lot of the time it wasn't anything at all. But, of course, being just nine years old, or maybe ten – I never have known just exactly how old I am – there wasn't much I could do to help out around a filling station. But I did keep the water barrel out in front filled and I swept out around the place and answered questions about how far it was to Cumberland Gap, and Corbin and Bristol and Gate City. Except for Gate City I had never been any of those places but Matt told me what to say. There weren't any schools around there but I didn't cotton much to going to school, anyway. Matt showed me how to read a little and how to do simple sums. I think he showed me all he knew about reading and writing and using figures, but it sure wasn't much.

Then one morning a truck loaded with lumber stopped in there with a bad tire. He wanted Matt to help him change it. They had to unload all the lumber before they could jack up the truck and then they had to load it back. It took about all day. Then when they were finished Matt leaned over to make one last check before the truck drove off. I guess the brakes slipped or something. Anyway, the truck rolled backwards and knocked Matt down. Before he could get out of the way the wheel passed over him. When we got him out of there even I knew he was dead.

They had to have an inquest and they kept the driver over for that. When it turned out to be an accident, pure and simple, they let him go. I asked him where he was going and he said Roanoke. I knew I was homeless again so I asked him to take me with him. It took most of two days and it turned out he was going just the other side of Roanoke. When he finally put me out I just started walking again. But this time I wasn't as scared as I had been two years before. I had grown a good bit. And I had saved all the money Matt ever gave me, and I had about $30 and I now knew what money was and what I could do with it. But one thing I knew not to do with it was spend any on bus fare. I just walked and now and then I hitched a ride. Just outside of a town called Waynesboro I was picked up by a farmer going back home after selling some pigs. He asked me about helping him out on his farm during the harvest since I didn't have no regular home. I figured I might as well. I wound up spending the winter there and on into the next summer. School started in July and run for several weeks so they could let the kids out long enough when the harvest came along to help out at home. When the farmer and his wife started talking about sending me to school I knew I had been there long enough. Once again I had saved my money and by now I had $55.

I walked and hitchhiked for a couple of days and wound up in a little town not far from Washington. It was getting dark and I was tired so I went into a place where I thought I could get something to eat. It turned out to be the first beer joint I was ever in.

By now I was about 13 years old but I was real big for my age. So a couple of older boys that was drinking beer just took to me real fast. That night I had my first taste of beer. I thought surely it would be my last one. It tasted awful and besides, it cost ten cents a bottle. But the upshot was that the fellows that I made friends with worked on a gang nearby that was building a road. They told me they could get me on if I wanted a job and I could make about $14 a week. Man, I jumped at the chance. I didn't know anybody in all the world made that much money. They told me I would have to lie about my age but that didn't bother me none. I just told the boss man I was 18 and he put me right to work.

I got a room at the same place the other fellows stayed. They tried to get me to go out with them at night but I didn't want to. But they kept after me and I finally went because I figured if they could get me a job they could also cause it to be taken away from me. But I didn't drink any more beer; at least not for the first few nights.

Then one Saturday night they got me to agree to go with them again. One of them had a car and they wanted me to go to Washington with them. I had spent a little money on some clothes, by far the best clothes I had ever had. I just had a coat and some pants and a shirt. The rest was overalls. Mostly I saved my money and by now I had over a hundred dollars.

When we got to Washington we went to a place they said was real good and we could have a hot time. It turned out to be just another beer joint. But there was girls in this one. And they talked me into trying beer again. This time I did manage to finish the whole bottle and I felt kind of warm inside. The girls kinda made over me and I thought I was really something. Even though I didn't have anything but a cheap coat and pants that matched a shirt, but no tie, they said I was real good looking. I guess I thought I had a real good time.

So the next Saturday, when they asked me to go with them again they didn't have to ask the second time. And they didn't have to beg me to be a sport and have a beer. I think I had been kinda looking forward to it. I didn't have but a couple of beers — maybe as many as three or four, but I just seemed to lose control of myself.

After while a fight broke out in the back of the place and me and my buddies crowded around to see what was happening. I don't know how I did it, but the first thing I knew I was in there swinging away, too.

Pretty soon the cops come and I was among those they took to jail. It was my second time in a jail, although I still wasn't quite

14, but claiming I was 18. Only this time the door wasn't left unlocked.

My buddies hightailed it back and left me stranded there. On Monday they took us into court. I got 30 days.

When I got out of the workhouse I was once again faced with the need to ponder my future a little. Fortunately, I had not lost my money in the fight, in the Washington jail or in the workhouse. I still had about $80 and my coat and pants.

Just before the bus that took us prisoners that was being released stopped to let us off in Washington we passed a big place that had a sign out in front that said "car hop wanted; meals, uniforms and good wages." I didn't know what a car hop was but I figured this was the job for me. A job that would give me my meals would save me some money. If they gave me uniforms I wouldn't have to spend any money on any more clothes than I had on. And the good wages sounded fine to me, even though I didn't know how much they would be. While I was in the workhouse I had worn jail clothes. And they cleaned my clothes and washed my shirt. So I figured I was presentable enough to go ask for that car hop job, even though I still had no idea what it was.

You told me one time, chaplain, that I could charm the birds right out of the tree when I wanted to. And I guess I can. The manager didn't much want to hire me. I had no references, at least none I was willing to give. I was dressed neatly enough, even if my clothes were cheap. But there must have been a lot of backwoods in me yet. I know I didn't talk nice like that manager did; not even as nice as most of the fellows I was in the workhouse with. I still don't talk so good, as you can see by this letter. But I must have done a whale of a piece of selling because I got the job.

They showed me how to be a car hop; how to run out and get the order when a car drove up. I had learned a little about counting from Matt and how to make change. The other car hops showed me the tricks of the trade, mainly about how to get good tips. Nobody showed me how to read the menu, though, or how to write it down when folks told me they wanted a cheeseburger. Christ, I didn't even know what a cheeseburger was. But I faked it out and I learned. I found out the bigger the order the better the tip and I also found out I had to have those tips because the "good wages" weren't but $10 a week. The boss was happy because I was getting good orders. I know it wasn't much, but to me it was a real big victory when I found out I could read every food item on that menu, even if I didn't know what some of the things were, like A-1 sauce, tartar sauce, and hot fudge sundaes and stuff like that.

Then it happened.

Us fellows that worked on the curb always had a bottle hidden away somewhere and when things were slow we had a little nip or two. On this particular night things were unusually slow and we emptied the first bottle and sent after another one. About midnight a car pulled into my station. I could tell the driver was pretty unsteady and the other man and the two women had been in the juice pretty good, too. It was a difficult order to take, not made any easier by the woman in the front seat making a play for me. To make a long story short, the driver — a big guy and pretty drunk by the time they were ready to leave, because he had been pulling on a bottle all the time they were there — kept giving me a hard time. He would blow his horn instead of flashing his lights for service, like the signs asked the customers to do. When I would get there he would want something like another ice cube in his water glass or a tooth pick. Most of all, he wanted to make smart cracks at me. And his woman kept making suggestive remarks. Pretty soon he was mad at me and her both. And my own short fuse was about burnt out, too. I was waiting on another car that had pulled in when they started to leave. It seemed like he turned his wheels so he could come straight at me as he gunned the motor and he turned just in time to keep from hitting me straight on. But he did brush me off and in my anxiety to get out of his way I made a dive for a grassy place on the side of the parking lot. The guy was pretty unsteady and lost control of the car and drove off on the grass on the other side of the pavement where the car came to a stop. He hadn't anymore than stopped when I had his door open and was pulling the driver out and whaling away at him. I had already messed him up pretty bad before anybody got to us to try to put a stop to the fight. It wasn't really a fight because I don't think he ever swung a punch and I didn't throw but five or six. But it was enough to break his jaw and his nose and he went to the hospital with a bad concussion. And I went to jail on a charge of felonious assault.

I got six months out of that. But while I was doing my time the manager of the place where I worked came to see me two or three times. He told me I had been a real good worker and the company was going to give me another chance when I got out. He was good to his word and the day after I finished doing my time I started car hopping again, but at another one of the drive-in's stores. That's where I met June, who was a waitress at the counter inside.

Pretty soon me and June had a real good thing going. Roosevelt had just been elected to his third term and Washington was humming with war talk. Lots of new people were coming to town and they were all spending money. Me and June were both raking in the tips. We started living together and right away she started all this talk about getting married. Hell, I didn't want any of that. I had everything I would have if I got married and none of the chains a preacher would tie to me.

One Saturday we both knocked off work after the lunch rush. Another couple and us hit a joint over in Georgetown and started with the boiler makers. You know, a straight shot with a beer chaser. Everybody was talking about the draft and going into the service for $21 a day once a month. You know that old song. The other guy said Hell; he was going to get married so the draft wouldn't get him. This seemed to make sense to me. I didn't think much of getting married but if it would keep me out of the draft and going over to let Hitler shoot at me it seemed like a pretty good idea. So by dark we was in the other guy's car heading for South Carolina where we could get married right away. I still wasn't but about 17 years old and the draft wouldn't have taken me if they knew my right age. But I had been faking my age, adding 3 or 4 years to it for so long I knew I would have a helluva time proving how old I really was.

It was a long night's drive. We had taken a couple of bottles along to keep us warm, we said. But we didn't drink an awful lot, I guess because we already had a pretty good glow on from the joint in Georgetown.

By the next morning we were in Charlotte, North Carolina, just a few miles from York, South Carolina, where we were going to get married. But it didn't seem like such a good idea now. We were all tired and the bottle didn't interest us anymore. We didn't want anything but to get something to eat and go to sleep. We found a place to get some ham and eggs and then we checked into a tourist home, each couple claiming to be man and wife, of course.

I woke up about the middle of the afternoon and found the other guy standing over our bed waving what was left of the other bottle. I guess he didn't go to sleep after all, because he was pretty high. He wanted us to have a drink. I didn't feel too good and I had heard plenty of times that a little drink then would fix you right up. It was all I could do to swallow the stuff but I got it down. All it did was make me to want more. Since there wasn't anymore I got up and put my clothes on and went out in the other guy's car. It didn't take long to find out where I could find a bottlegger out on the highway north where we had just come from early that morning. I paid him about half the money I had left for two fifths of whiskey and headed back to the tourist home. All of us had a few drinks and we must have got pretty loud because the landlady came and told us we would have to get out.

By then we all thought that getting married was a pretty good idea after all. So we found the road to York and got there about eleven o'clock that night and woke the justice of the peace up. We got the knot tied and headed back to Washington. We was all supposed to go to work the next day but we knew now there wasn't any way to make it. But we kept trying. By now we was down to $10 among the four of us after we got the gas tank filled up.

When we got to High Point, North Carolina, we was out of liquor again and all of us had a big thirst going. After asking a few questions we found another bootlegger on the road out to Greensboro, which was the way we were going anyway. That took $6 of the last $10 and the gas tank was getting low again.

Just outside of Danville, Virginia, we blew a tire. The other guy and I put the spare on and found it was about ready to blow, too. When we got through Danville we found an all-night gas station and pulled in and bought a tire. Then we pulled over to the gas pump and told the guy to fill it up. I was driving. We watched the gauge and when it showed about three-quarters full I hit the starter and the engine caught right away and we were out of that place and on the road before the gas station guy could pick himself up off the ground and get the gas pump stopped. So we still had $4, enough gas to get home on and a couple more drinks apiece.

We kept thinking about what if that jerk back at the gas station had got our license number and phoned it into the state police. So we got out and bent the plate so it couldn't be read easy. But there wasn't anything we could do to hide the kind of car we was driving.

Right after we passed through a little town about 50 miles above Danville, I saw in the rear view mirror that a car had pulled out of a side road behind us and was picking up speed fast. I figured it was the law so I pushed the throttle to the floor. It was pretty hilly and there were a lot of curves, I went into one of the curves faster than we could make it. I don't know what all happened. I remember turning over at least once and maybe several times before the car left the road, still turning over. I come to lying on the ground down the side of the hill, or mountain or whatever it was. I knew things were bad but I didn't want to make any signs of being conscious and having to talk before I knew how bad they were. So I faked still being out. I was hurting pretty bad but I felt like I could get up and walk if I had to. There was one policeman — I guess the one that was driving the car that chased us — and two or three other people around I later learned were passing motorists. When I figured there wasn't anybody watching me I tried to look around and see where the others were. About half-way back up the road I saw something that looked like a body covered with an old rain coat. Close by was another mound just like it. That accounted for two of my companions and I figured they were dead. I figured right. But I could hear a siren coming up the road before I found out where the other one was. One of the truck drivers had an axe or something beating on what was left of the car. There sure wasn't much left; — it looked like a piece of tin roof that had blown off a barn. Then he reached underneath a mass of wreckage and when he finally turned around I heard him say, "She's dead, too. Just that one fellow down there is still alive."

When the ambulance got there I kept on playing unconscious while I tried to figure things out. Finally, it came to me that there wasn't but one thing to do. The next day when they questioned me I told them I was in the back seat asleep when the accident happened. I told them the other guy was driving. Since the state cop that was chasing us hadn't seen who was driving there wasn't any way they could prove it was me. They brought the gas station fellow into to try to prove I was driving, since he identified me as the driver when we run out of his station without paying for an $11 tire and $4 worth of gas. There must have been some kind of angel riding on my shoulder because the Commonwealth Attorney decided there wasn't enough evidence to prosecute me for manslaughter by car. But when they charged me with larceny for running off without paying for the gas and the tire that angel took off and I did a year in the pen.

By the time I got out the war was going real good. I made my way back to Washington. I was broke, of course. But my old landlady had kept my other clothes. I must have done some more charming because I talked her into letting me have a clean suit, shirt and a pair of shoes with a promise of paying up the rent as soon as I got a payday. That took some doing because I didn't even have a job.

I went back to my old boss. He had always kind of had a liking for me; said that when I put myself to it I was the best worker he ever had and the smartest. He didn't think much of putting me back to work now. But there was such a help shortage he finally gave me one more chance. But he told me to watch my step especially well and if he ever heard of me so much as drinking a beer he would fire me on the spot. Since the war was going on and there wasn't any gas much the car-hopping business was out so he put me inside the restaurant waiting on tables. And that was where I was when the draft got me. With my kind of background, my lack of education and not even knowing excactly how old I really was it didn't seem like they ought to have taken me. But I guess the Army needed men awful bad.

I was a good soldier when I had to be or when I wanted to be. But there were times when I could get by with less than my best. And there were times when I just plain didn't want to be a good soldier. I made it up to buck sergeant four times and got busted three. Spent a lot of time on restriction or in the guard house. But I saw a lot of action, too. A helluva lot.

I got sent back to the States late in 1945 to Camp Pendleton. I wasn't there but about four weeks. But that was long enough to meet Rosemary and marry her.

When I got out of the service we went back to Washington and I was lucky again. I got my old job back and I kept my nose good and clean. Inside a year I had been made assistant night manager of the biggest restaurant in the chain. Rosemary and I got an apartment out in Silver Spring. But she bugged me awful bad about wanting me to give her my paycheck every week. I wound up giving her most of it most of the time and she squirreled it away. She got a job, too, and she was the savingest girl I ever saw. We would go out on Saturday nights once in a while and take on a few drinks. She would let me have a beer at home once in a while during the week but beyond this she seriously limited my drinking. Considering how short our courtship was I guess we got along better than we were supposed to. But my natural way of getting in trouble fixed that up.

After the restaurant closed up one morning about 2 o'clock one of the regular late night customers was in there drinking coffee. He asked me if I had ever been out to Jimmy's place, a gambling joint that was located half in the District and half in Maryland. He said there was a couple big games going on out there and asked me to go with him and look in on them and maybe sit in for a while. So I went along.

I pretty well broke even that night, or morning it was because it was eight o'clock when I rolled into the apartment. Rosemary was some kind of mad. I guess that's why it didn't take any talking at all to get me to go back out to Jimmy's that night. And I couldn't do anything wrong; I couldn't do anything but win. So I came away $900 richer than when I went in. I was hooked.

Every chance I had after that I was at Jimmy's gambling. I don't know why but the place was never raided even though it seemed like everybody knew it was there. I had a fantastic run of luck Six weeks after I started going there I had a new Buick and a new Dodge, both bought at post-war black market prices. But a week later, when I left there one night – or one morning – I had to borrow carfare from Jimmy.

Needless to say, Rosemary took a very dim view of all this. She wouldn't even drive the Dodge I bought for her; it just sat on the parking lot until I lost it.

As soon as I had another payday or two, I started going back out to Jimmy's every chance I got, trying to get lucky again. I either broke even or just lost or won a little. There weren't any more hot streaks. It got so I was working about nine hours every day, sleeping about five and spending the rest of the time at Jimmy's. You know this didn't go well with Rosemary. After one specially bad morning I had a few drinks on the way home. I was in a foul mood. Rosemary hadn't gone to work that morning so she started in on me. I had never hit her before but this time I beat her up.

That night the manager at the restaurant wanted to get away a little early. He put most of the money in the safe and told me to lock up the rest in the strongbox in the office when we closed up.

I had got myself into hock to a lot of fellows around and had no cash of my own other than carfare to and from work for the rest of the week. I told myself I felt lucky that night. Besides, if I went out to Jimmy's and had a hot streak of luck it would really show Rosemary. So instead of putting the money in the strongbox, I put the bills in my pocket – about $300. I figured I would leave Jimmy's a little early that morning, before the day manager came on at the restaurant, and I would slip by there and put the money in the strongbox and nobody would be the wiser. Well, I never won a pot. In two hours I was broken. It wasn't a crooked game; Jimmy didn't allow that kind of thing. I just couldn't repeat my lucky streak.

When I got home Rosemary wasn't there. She left me a note to say she could put up with a lot of things but the one thing she wouldn't stand was me beating up on her.

I knew I had to find Rosemary. I had counted on what she had saved to get the money to pay back the restaurant. I knew I couldn't get it until after the bank opened at 9:30, which would be long after the day manager found out some of the money was gone. But I figured I could bluff my way out of it, saying I had just forgot to put the bills in the box. I hadn't had any trouble since I came back from the war and what I had before didn't have anything to do with being short in my money. I figured I could ride it out if I could just find Rosemary and get the bank book. But I couldn't find her. And the bank wouldn't let me have any of the money without it.

All that day I stayed away from the apartment because I figured they would be looking for me. And, of course, I couldn't go to work that night. Rosemary hadn't gone to work that day and none of her friends knew where she was or they wouldn't tell me. It was the same all the next day.

Finally, I figured the only thing to do was to go back and find the boss and make a clean breast of everything and ask for a chance to work it out. But it was too late. There was already a warrant out for me, charging me with embezzlement. My good life had just gone down the drain. Since there wasn't any policeman there, they couldn't arrest me right then.

I was dirty by then and had a two-day beard. I decided I would try the back way into the apartment and get a bath, a shave, a chance of clothes, and whatever I could carry out of there to the hock shop to get enough money to try to slip out of town. I hadn't been able to find Rosemary anywhere else but I found her there, packing the rest of her things.

I told her about the jam I was in. She said she was leaving me but that she had planned to get in touch with me and divide everything we had with me right down the middle. That meant that my half of the savings account would come to over a thousand dollars. She didn't want to do it but I finally begged her to get out of there and go get my half and bring it to me right then. Meantime, I wouldn't answer the door or the phone while she was gone.

101

When she got back I was ready to go out again. So I went back to the restaurant with the $300 and begged the manager to take it and drop the charge against me. He said it was out of his hands and he couldn't do a thing. I was going to be arrested, he said. So I made a beeline out of there and across town where I thought I would be safer from the cops looking for me, and I could think over what I ought to do. It was then that I decided to try to call my old boss, who was now a district manager, and get him to help me. I located him pretty fast. He already knew about the jam I was in. But he just didn't seem to want to help me anymore. But I begged and pleaded with him and he finally agreed to see what he could do. He told me to call him back in about two hours since there wasn't any place he could call me.

I felt like a hunted animal. It seemed like I shouldn't stay in one place too long. So I went out and got on a streetcar and rode to the end of the line. I changed and got on a bus and started out in another direction. One time when the bus stopped a policeman got on. I grabbed a newspaper somebody had left on the seat beside me and pretended to read it, although I still couldn't read too good. I felt like that cop was looking right at me and I kept wondering when he was going to put the pinch on me. After a real long time I finally peeked around the side of the paper and the cop was gone.

When I got to the end of that line I found a phone and called my old boss again. He told me to meet him at police headquarters and he would fix everything up for me.

That police sergeant sure didn't want to withdraw the warrant. He kept lecturing me and giving the boss a hard time. But the boss said he might as well tear the warrant up because there wouldn't be anybody from the company to testify against me. So I was free again. But I was out of a job; my wife was leaving me, and I just didn't know which way to go.

I spent the next couple of days in beer joints and in a cheap hotel. I decided to go find Rosemary and see if we couldn't patch things up and try again. I went to where she worked and at first she wouldn't see me. But when she decided I just wasn't going to leave without seeing her she came out. But there was fire in her eyes and her mind was made up. She called me an ignorant bum and said I didn't have anything on my mind but gambling and now I was staying drunk along with it. She was right on all points and I was just drunk enough to take another poke at her; a real good one. Then I ran out and went to the bus station and got on the first bus out of town.

I didn't know where I was going, but the bus just happened to be going south. After riding all day and half the night I got off in a little town to try and get me something to eat. I found an all-night hash house where the waiter was a mouthy sort of guy. Turned out he was the owner.

I still had a couple hundred dollars so there wasn't any pressure on me. When I finished eating I went out and found me a room in the little hotel and slept until the middle of the next afternoon.

I got up and went out and ate again. After that I just walked around. I found a beer joint and went in to enjoy my favorite pastime, drinking.

This went on for a couple of days and finally one night I wound up in the same joint where I had eaten the first night I got there. The guy was talkative again. Said he needed a counter man for the night shift so he could go back on days. I figured this was a way to pay my expenses since I knew I was going to run out of money sometime soon.

I hadn't worked there long until a couple of guys came in early one morning and I knew when they stepped in they were looking for trouble. Kept calling me "pretty boy." I "pretty boyed" them; with my fists. Like always before, I didn't know when to stop and they carted those fellows off to the hospital. I got 30 days for it. When I got out I hung around town for a few days and caught another bus. This time I just went 30 or 40 miles down the road because I didn't want to spend too much on bus tickets.

I couldn't find a job in a hash house. But there was a brick yard here and that's what they put me to doing when I went to the workhouse for cleaning up that beer joint in Washington years before.

When payday came I went out with a couple of fellows and the first thing I knew I was drunk and in another fight. And then I was in jail again, this time for 10 days. When I got out they took me back on at the brickyard. But two paydays later there was another big drunk and another big fight. This time I got 90 days and they wouldn't take me back on at the brickyard this time.

Once again I got on the bus and went another few miles down the road. This time I got a job in another diner. The owner's wife took a shine to me and that was OK with me. But her husband caught us in bed together. I don't know how bad I beat him up because I was on another bus 20 minutes after he walked in the door. That's when I came to your town.

When I went out to the plant and asked for a job I wasn't trained to do any of the better jobs. But they did put me on as a laborer. And that's all I could do; there wasn't any more money left out of what Rosemary gave me to buy another bus ticket. Not long after that I came to you.

After I told you my life history up to that time you asked me again about how much I had been to church. I told you I didn't know anything about going to church or praying or any of that kind of stuff. I remember during the war when I was in the Army Air Corps and coming back after a bombing mission with three engines out and the fourth one just sputtering. There were holes shot into every part of that plane and we were losing altitude fast and the landing gear was shot out. All the other guys were down on their knees praying and all I could do was cuss myself for not staying in the infantry.

I don't remember much about what we talked about on that first visit but I know I felt a lot better after that.

The next day I came back again. I asked you about this praying business. I don't guess I'll ever forget what you said then. You said, "Let's start by talking about the greatest prayer of all time, the Lord's Prayer." You were a little shocked, I think, to learn that I never even knew anything about the Lord's Prayer. So you began to read it and explain it to me.

"Our Father, who art in heaven," you said. Then you explained that this is a kind of salutation that makes us realize that there is an everlasting power much greater than any man; a power that can lift us up even when everything else tries to hold us down.

"Hallowed be Thy name." And you said this is a kind of acknowledgement of God's greatness and his powers.

"Thy Kingdom come." This, you said, was a plea that God's goodness be greater than the evil that drives men.

"Thy Will be Done, on Earth as it is in Heaven." This part bothered me a little even after you explained it to me. I couldn't understand how, if God's will can be done on earth just by asking Him that it be that way, then how come people that knew more than me and could ask it this way — then why did people just keep on getting in trouble. But you had won me over and I was willing to believe it just because you said it.

"Give us this day our daily bread." You said this was asking God, not only to feed us, but to give us the strength and courage and wisdom to do the things we need to do every day so the problems of the day won't bug us too much.

"And forgive us our debts as we forgive our debtors." I couldn't quite understand this. Why should I forgive somebody that doesn't pay me what he owes me? But you said it didn't quite mean that; that it means asking God to treat us like we treat our fellow men; that if we want better treatment from God, we ought to treat our fellow men better.

"And lead us not into temptation, but deliver us from evil." This, you said, was asking God to turn us around when we walked into a situation where we might hurt somebody else, or get drunk or beat somebody up, or do something else that is wrong.

"For thine is the Kingdom, and the Power and the Glory, forever, Amen." You said this was admitting that man, after all, isn't the most powerful thing, that all our power comes from God. You said it was like admitting that if we turn our lives and our wills over to God, everything will come out fine, even if sometimes we don't think so at the time.

All this just made me want to come back to you for more. Pretty soon I was in your office about every minute I wasn't on the job.

About the girl I was in trouble with, things looked pretty rough. But you said God never promised to make things easy for us; He just offers us a source from which we can gather all the strength we need to face the hardest task if we just ask Him and let Him help us in His own way.

Well, I just went down and knocked on his door and talked with the girl's father. He wasn't very big but he started out by taking a big poke at me. I dodged it and the next one and the next one. When he fell down swinging at me I helped him back to his feet. He must have known I could have beat him to a pulp if I just wanted to. But he kept swinging away and I would pick him up when he lost his balance. Pretty soon he was all worn out. So while he sat there on the ground trying to get his breath I told him I was real sorry about what had happened to his daughter. I told him I thought I already had a wife so I couldn't marry her. But, I told him, I would pay her medical expenses, or as much of them as I could and pay the rest later. And I would support the baby after it came.

I guess he must have known I wanted to do the right thing because after he got his breath he didn't seem mad anymore. When she started going to the doctor regularly I went by and paid her bills and I bought what little medicine she needed. And I helped her buy what she would need for the baby after it came.

It wasn't as hard as it looked like it would be to start because, honestly, Chaplain, it seemed like I had some kind of new strength I never had before. I wanted to do right a whole lot more than I wanted to do wrong. It was that way on my job, too. Pretty soon they made me foreman of the work gang with a good increase in pay.

Me and the girl's father actually got to be pretty good friends. When her time came, she went away to another town to have the baby and she put it up for adoption. When she came back her father told me I didn't owe her or him anything else. Besides, he said, it was about as much her fault as it was mine. I just happened to get caught instead of some other guy. Pretty soon she left town and the last I heard she had gone to some school to learn to be a beauty operator and she was getting along pretty good now.

I was going to school, too. You urged me to get into the night classes the company sponsored. I had never really gone to school before. I had a few months, I guess, in the sorry little school back in Virginia's mountains when I was a kid. But I hadn't learned anything but what letters and numbers looked like; I never learned except for experiences with Matt, and then as a car hop, in the Army and back in the restaurant in Washington, how to put them together. I had to take a test and it said that I had a real high intelligence. I guess that's why I learned so fast and in a year or two I got my "equivalency high school diploma," they called it.

Then after you kept after me to do it I took some other courses and got to know a lot about the company's business. That's when the promotions really started coming.

All the time you kept talking to me about God, and God's way. You helped me to learn to read the bible. I thought that was an awful lot different from reading anything else. But you showed me how to understand it.

I met Georgia then and it was love at first sight. She was active in church work and I went right along with her. I knew I wanted to marry her. So, with your help, I made the necessary contacts that eventually put me back in touch with Rosemary. She had got a divorce and was remarried. So I was now free to marry Georgia.

Then the company opened up in the midwest and asked me if I wanted to go out there and manage their new installation. I wasn't sure about myself, but Georgia and I talked it over with you and you said that, first of all, the company wouldn't have offered it to me if they hadn't thought I could handle the job. Second, you said, "All things are possible in God." You told me that if I would just do the best I could every single day, and constantly ask for God's help, I would get along fine. And I did. For a while, anyway.

Out there I fell in with some other fellows that had made it pretty good with their companies. They told me about how some of the guys were making it big in uranium stocks and they showed me how to do it. All there was to it was to watch out for announcements of new issues. It was awful cheap, sometimes just a penny a share. So I would buy a few hundred shares when a new announcement came along that looked good. If it went up to two cents I would sell out and double my money in just a few days. Man, that was great. The good salary I was getting, plus the money I was making on uranium stock put me right in with the country club set. But that put me back in close contact with the bars.

One night I went out there on my way home after a particularly hard day. Not only had things gone wrong all day at the plant, but for the past several weeks the uranium stocks hadn't done what they ought to do. It was just like when my luck went sour at Jimmy's gambling house in Washington years before. I couldn't win for losing. It just seemed like the thing to do for me to have a drink at the club. Of course, they took me home drunk. If this wasn't bad enough, it happened again just a few days later. This scared us real bad, especially Georgia. I felt like when I got out here with a real good job and making a lot of money in the stock market I was too good to take my problems to anybody else so I hadn't had any real good friends like you I could talk to. So we made a special trip back to see you. We told you all that had happened. Then you went back to something I had read in the Bible, about not being able to serve two masters. You said that my job, my wife and my God were my real Master, all rolled into one. You said that when I got to playing the stock market and attaching so much importance to money, social position and the country club set I was trying to serve more than one master and that was where I was getting in trouble.

So we went back out to the midwest. I cut out the stock market manipulations. I tried to get out of the country club crowd but that wasn't so easy.

I had a lot of tensions then. Things just didn't seem to make much sense anymore. I kind of dropped out of church and stopped reading my Bible. Then you stopped to see me when you passed through town. After that I tried again to read my Bible and to pray like you taught me to. I even sat down and wrote out all the things you had said to me that was most meaningful, including your explanation of the Lord's Prayer. It helped, but pretty soon I was thinking again about all the money I used to make in the uranium stock market. I began to stop off at the club again to talk with my old buddies there to see if there was anything new to put a little money in and make more on the side. Of course, stopping in the bar meant taking more drinks which I should have known by then just led to more grief. All my humility was gone. I couldn't understand what I was reading any more so I stopped reading the Bible. I thought God wasn't answering my prayers so I stopped praying. Then one night one of the fellows at the bar said something I didn't like and two seconds later he was on the floor with a broken jaw.

Once again we went to see you. This thing at the club got hushed up but the rumors floated around and eventually got back to the company. I admitted everything and management was willing to go along with me for another chance. You told me to go off somewhere and try to think things out objectively. You told me the reason it didn't seem like God was answering my prayers was that I started out with an attitude like I might be saying, "Look here, God, this is what I want so you do it." You told me that the people that worked for me were responsible to me and I could give them orders. But that I was God's servant and I not only took orders from Him, but I should *look* for orders from Him in the form of guidance. So back to the middle west we went.

But somehow or other I couldn't get around that fierce pride of mine. I couldn't reconcile myself to getting along very well on what I made with the company instead of twice as much, like it used to be when I was playing with uranium stock. I brooded more and more and more and it seemed like the only thing to do was drink. And when I drank I got drunk and got rough. Eventually I got in another fight and about killed the other fellow. This time the company didn't give me another chance.

Inside a year everything we had was gone. I went from one poor job to an even worse one and then no jobs at all. One day I was sitting at home with a bottle of cheap wine, one of an endless chain of such bottles. It was a sorry, shabby little place. We wouldn't have it, I don't guess, if Georgia hadn't gone to work as a waitress. But she hadn't gone to work this day. I had got to where I was taking my bitterness out on her. I was always taking punches at her. Sometime the night before I got a good one in and her eye was swollen closed. I was thinking about the big house we used to have. The big salary. The big money that uranium stocks poured in for a while. On the table were four or five letters from you I had never even opened. They were several months old and some had been forwarded. But the last time we moved we left no forwarding address because I didn't want creditors or anybody else to know where to find me. Georgia asked me why I didn't open them and see what you had to say. I told her to mind her own business. She retreated into her little shell and for some reason it infuriated me. I hit her just one time real good and got my half-empty bottle of cheap wine and another full one and went down into the basement. I woke up the next morning in a cell. They said I had beat my wife to death.

Maybe I did. I don't know. But I didn't beat her all at one time. If I killed her I did it a blow at a time. The first blow was when I lost my humility when things were going so good. The next one was when I lost everything you ever taught me to believe, and tried to be my own master. Then there were blows with my fist. If I killed her, it was one blow at a time. Just like life knocked me out one blow at a time. But it didn't have to be that way. Just like I ducked the blows of the angry father of the girl I got pregnant, I could have ducked life's hard blows just by retreating behind all the things you taught me about God's love and His help if only I would ask for it and believe in Him.

The best road map in the world won't do you any good if you don't pay any attention to it. If you don't do what the map says you will surely get lost.

You gave me a real good map. When I followed it I got along real good. I think one of the best things the company does is having you there to help dopes like me out. That way we do our jobs better. But then I not only started disregarding the map you made me; I threw it away. And, oh boy, did I get lost!

They will be coming to get me soon. I'm sorry this is such a long letter but I didn't have anything else to do but sit here and think. And like I said, I still don't talk too good and I guess that means I can't write so good, either.

Thanks again for all you did for me. I'm sorry about throwing the map away because I believe now if people will just follow that map they can go anywhere they want to go if God wills it. I just wish that I — — — . Never mind. They are here now.

CHAPTER X

"YOU DON'T HAVE TO STAY AS YOU ARE"

If you wish to be miserable, you must think about yourself; about what you want, what you like, what respect people ought to pay you, and then to you nothing will be pure. You spoil everything you touch; you will make sin and misery out of everything God sends you. You can be as wretched as you choose.
— *Charles Kingsley*

There is no man so low down that the cure for his condition does not lie strictly within himself.
— *T. L. Masson*

Many times the chaplain meets the viewpoint that life can't be changed. Everyone needs to know his life can be changed. To offset this attitude the following information is given to those counselled.

If you thought when you awoke this morning that today was going to be just another day, you were mistaken.

Today is different.

Although you may not realize it yet, something wonderful, something powerful — and perhaps a little frightening and strange — has happened, or is about to happen to you.

Before this day is over, a miracle can occur in your life. Indeed, that miracle already has begun to materialize. It started when you decided that you are not satisfied with yourself, and resolved, moreover, to do something about it.

You made such a decision, consciously or unconsciously, when you picked up this book and began to read. You may have reached that decision on the spur of the moment, or you may have brooded about it for days, weeks, or months. However it happened, you set in motion the first in a chain of events which, if you will permit them to develop, will have a profound influence on your life.

You may be rich or poor, healthy or ill, male or female, adult or teenager, saint or sinner. Who you are, what you are, or what you have been are not incalculably important. The significant thing is that you are not satisfied with being as you are, and want to become something better.

Here, then, is good news for you:

YOU DON'T HAVE TO STAY AS YOU ARE.

No matter what your problems — your troubles, limitations, weaknesses, excesses, failures, disappointments, misfortune, bad breaks; whatever your age, sex, race, nationality, marital status, financial standing, religious preference — you can wipe the slate clean and start writing a new diary about a new YOU!

I say, again, you already have changed.

The simple fact that you admitted to yourself that you were on the wrong course constituted a major change in your way of thinking, and consequently, in your life. Before today, you may have been too vain, too selfish, too proud or too arrogant to admit that you were drifting along in the wrong direction, or seemingly in no direction at all. Now you want to discover that elusive star that lights the way to an authentic and meaningful life.

Have heart. That star DOES shine. You can pluck it from the

heavens and make it shine for you.

"How?" you ask. "How can I, who have never succeeded at anything, make a success of my miserable life? How can a nobody become a somebody?" This is the place where you are going to be asked to begin with a new self image. For some reason you have accepted a self image that has blocked your emotional, intellectual and spiritual progress. This has brought you to a disillusionment with life and yourself. Thank God. This is where all newness of life begins.

You must proceed by plan. You must first determine wherein you are lacking. You must then determine what you want to be. Finally, you must chart a new course and get your life moving in the right direction. Picture in your mind the kind of person that you want to be and rid yourself of that which you don't want. There is a power in positive thinking to get you started.

If you were overhauling an engine, you would first take it apart, piece by piece, and determine which parts needed replacement or repair. You must examine yourself, as you would inspect an engine, to discover your faults. After you have sorted out the shortcomings or weaknesses, you must discard them, or learn how to deal with them. With proper plan, you can then make of yourself a whole person, capable of going as fast and as far as you are willing to strive for self-improvement.

But before you can improve yourself, you must first understand the nature of your being. You must examine every facet of your person — the physical, the mental, the moral, the spiritual. *There must be purpose in your desire to be different than you are, and you must strive to bring about the changes* that can fill your life with joy.

"But I haven't the moral strength, the courage, the willpower or the intelligence to do all these things," you may say. "That is why I have failed before, and shall fail again."

Nonsense.

You have an inner strength you have never dreamed of. You have inner resources never before tapped, and you can find a friend who will never desert you. He will always be working to bring you to your highest and best potentiality.

Don't sell yourself short. One man's capabilities are pretty much like another's. It's what they do with them that counts.

"A man ain't nothin' but a man," said John Henry, the legendary "steel-drivin' man."

You'd be surprised how close to the truth old John hit when he swung that little hammer.

First of all, God didn't take time to create a bunch of kooks, nuts, hippies, and mixed-up kids.

They made themselves that way.

God created man in His image. Therefore, all men at birth are what God made them. There are certain genetic differences, to be sure. In some cases, they represent man's effort to improve the strain — or at least not to weaken it. Basically, however man has but little control over the natural attributes of his offspring. All the planning in the world — the selection of a mate, the pre-natal care of the mother, the plans for the unborn child — cannot insure that the baby will be healthy, happy, and normal. Nor does the mating of two peasants mean that a prince will not be born of the union. Many a genius has been born in the most humble of surroundings. Some of the greatest statesmen, writers, musicians, painters, poets, doctors, lawyers, ministers, scientists, teachers, came from impoverished or broken homes. On the other hand, our prisons abound with men and women who had every material advantage their parents could offer. Our mental institutions have many inmates who have disregarded their God-given opportunities to be well. From their family background, they could have had anything their hearts desired.

The success or failure of a man is not determined by the circumstances of his birth. It does not depend upon his God-given talents, but almost entirely upon whether he uses them for good or evil. Of all God's creations, man alone has the power of reason, the intelligence to distinguish between right and wrong, the ability to understand what he is, and what God would have him be. If he fails, it is because he made the wrong choices and commitments. He has become a victim of his own low self esteem. Everyone has this low esteem until he begins to change it through the ways suggested in this book. Man has compromised his conscience and become enmeshed in the web of defeat and despair. He can correct these wrong choices through responsibility, reality, right choices, repentance and confession, and a religious life.

Because he cannot wait to get out into the world and stand on his own two feet, man terminates his formal education, and lives to regret it. Because he sees in marriage the fulfillment of desires he does not really understand, he makes an early and inadvisable marriage and ends up making himself, his wife, and his children miserable. Because he is master of his household, the man who buys the groceries and pays the bills, handles all his own affairs, depends on nobody but himself, he thinks he can manage his life without the help of God. He does not teach his children to say their prayers, ask for blessing at the dinner-table, read the Bible or go to church, and his children are left without that nearness to God that only children have. Their lives can become joyful, useful and full only when they become mature enough to figure things out for themselves.

This may not be your picture, but you have a similar portrait of yourself that you are responsible for reshaping. A plastic surgeon does more than alter the outward appearance, he must also alter the man's inner self. You cooperate by thinking of what you want to become. Right now decide you will accept responsibility for what you are and what you are going to be. You are tempted to blame your shortcomings on everybody and everything except yourself. You must permit yourself to understand that whatever you are, or what you may eventually become, depends on nobody or nothing but you. There never was a time when you had no choice in the direction you would take. You have never neglected a duty, committed a sin, walked away from a responsibility, succumbed to an exciting temptation, but which you could have overcome by simply saying "no" to yourself. The basic cause of all neurosis is irresponsible behavior, the failure to make right choices in the strategic areas of life.

It is altogether true that you are what you made of yourself. It is equally true that you can, from this moment, make of yourself anything you want to be.

If you want to be a poet, start by writing a poem. If you want to be a singer, sing. If you want to be a scholar, study. If you want to be a preacher, start by preparing your life in God's will. If you want to be an executive, or a foreman, or a superintendent, start by mastering the smallest details of your business. When you have mastered most of them, a better job will be waiting for you. If you want your marriage to be a happy one, start by being honest with your mate. Be as pleasant, as kind, as loving, as considerate, as attentive, as appreciative as you were during your courtship, and your honeymoon will last forever.

There is a widespread and popular contention that once a pattern of behavior has been established in a man, he cannot change.

Such a theory, no matter how scientifically arrived at and substantiated, is hogwash.

It may be true of a mule. "You can change a fool, but a

doggone mule is a mule until he dies," goes a muleskinner song.

Here, the mule is indomitable; the "fool" capable of change.

It is true, perhaps, that some people don't CHANGE. But man definitely has the power at hand to CHANGE HIMSELF. This is a power God makes available to all who will receive it, and learn how to apply this strength daily to his life. Herein lies the agony and the ecstasy.

If a mother's prayers could change her son or daughter, there would be no drunkards, immorality, drug addicts, thieves, prostitutes, criminals, atheists, madmen or murderers. Almost inevitably, man falls or fails IN SPITE of the efforts and concern of the people closest to him. A man will be influenced, of course, by the teachings of his parents when he was young, and by the company he keeps when he becomes a man. But in the end, man reserves for himself the right of making his own decisions. Sometimes he insists on that privilege to the point that he rejects or ignores the advice of others purely to protest their interference in his affairs. His desire to be completely self-propelled causes him to crash dive his life into a hell of his own making.

If you have the power to decide for yourself how you will manage your life, it is equally true that you are responsible for your success or failure. Before you can tap your inner resources — the power within you to change — you must come to a full realization that you made yourself what you are today.

You may have been persuaded to the contrary. There is a popular theory among psychologists, psychiatrists, ministers and other professionals who deal clinically with human misery and failure that emotional instability and irresponsibility are one and the same, and constitute a "medical" rather than a "moral" problem. In other words, the socially irresponsible person is ill, and should be treated by a doctor, as in any illness. He should be nursed back to health and normality with "tender, loving care," with the understanding that he was not responsible for his behavior. It is the belief of the authors that these are moral problems not medical.

The outstanding psychiatrist Carl Jung found through his long years of counseling that every person had basically a religious problem. In his *Modern Man in Search of a Soul*, he states,

"Among all my patients in the second half of life, that is to say over thirty-five, there has not been one whose problem in the last resort has not been that of finding a religious outlook on life. It is safe to say that every one of them fell ill because he had lost that which the living religions of every age have given their followers, and none of them have been really healed who did not regain his religious outlook."

Behaviorists contend, for instance, that alcoholism is an illness.

Any medical approach which does not involve morality in its diagnosis and treatment of "illness" induced or produced by human behavior, is too negative to be altogether convincing. When a person is told that he is not responsible for being as he is, there is a corresponding inference that he also is incapable of being anything different. That simply is not true, in most cases, and encouraging such an evasion of responsibility is more destructive than restorative.

A great many scientifically oriented people – in medicine, psychology, theology, sociology, criminology, penology, – are changing to the moral viewpoint.

As far back as 1936, Anton T. Boisen suggested that it is a colossal and costly mistake to regard emotionally disturbed and socially irresponsible people as ill. Two West Coast psychiatrists, Dr. William Glasser and Dr. G. L. Harrington with their Reality Therapy, believe there is no such thing as mental illness, but moral irresponsibility. Glasser states that people do not act irresponsibly because they are ill, but that they are ill because they act irresponsibly. Integrity Therapy expounded by Dr. Hobart Mowrer puts all healing of emotional problems in the area of moral guilt. Confession to "significant others" releases these surpressed tensions, and following restitution for failure, enables the individual to resume his life as an authentic, responsible person.

Great emotional conflict is the consequence of compromising the conscience again and again until one becomes something he did not intend to be. A reasonable, mellow, and friendly personality apparently is trying to emerge from many hostile, emotionally upset people.

A British psychologist, Hans J. Eyseuck, has shown through clinical research that treatment based on the medical approach did not bring emotionally disturbed persons a more measurable recovery than that of similar patients who received no treatment at all.

You don't necessarily have to come to the brink of emotional, mental, or physical disaster for your life to be a failure. If you are less than you are capable of being, you need to manage and discipline yourself, and rise to the heights you are capable of ascending. One pinnacle will inspire you to proceed to a higher slope, and you will continue to climb mountains as long as there are mountains to conquer. The final summit is "Perfection," and you will not attain it, but your desire to conquer it, and your discontentment with any lesser achievement will keep you on the high ground.

Any person who is totally satisfied with himself is a quitter. Or he aspired to nothing, and attained it.

All improvement and progress in an individual or a nation are motivated by discontentment and desire.

> Margueritte Harmon Bro penned these lines:
> "Of course we long to be more than we are. Why is it that no matter how much outward success we have there is still restless, gnawing, unrelenting desire to become more than we are?"
>
> The same concept was expressed by Gerald Heard:
> "A man has by his striving become conscious, as he becomes aware of his need to experience, to learn, to understand, he must, if he is true to his inner need to fulfill his true nature, grasp the reasons why it is in his nature to strive, to seek, to find; his condition has aligned him for his destiny, what forces have energized him for his effort, what goals his trained power could attain – He is drawn by a dream of a future of yet undisclosed excellence."

No one can honestly blame someone else for what he is, or why he believes as he does. Many people declare they have been mistreated, misunderstood, or rejected, and can never forget it. They say they have been taught certain things which they have not been able to overcome. But they can, if they will never quit trying.

Quitters never win, and winners never quit.

It is not the number of times you falter, fail, or fall – but the times you get up and keep going that count.

There is no human failure that cannot be atoned by subsequent success. You can correct any mistake, repent of any sin, transform weakness into strength. But you must first admit that you are wrong. Believe that there is God – who can make more out of your life than you can. Believe that you can discover how to get His power into your life. If God holds the key to life and hidden inner resources, aren't you foolish not to appropriate this key?

Man's stubborn insistence that he is right, when there is no way of knowing that he is entirely right, is his greatest defeat. Walter Lippman related that truth to history when he wrote: "The damage done by years of adherence to decaying ideas is very great."

People get into all kinds of involvements and sins because they will not be honest with themselves. The unwillingness to face the truth about themselves causes many people to live unhappy, maladjusted lives, in constant conflict, always fearing that what they really are will be found out. Being honest about motives is a basic secret of the good life — which is nothing more than a healthy, happy relationship between oneself, God, and one's fellowman.

There is much joy in the searching and in finding the real person and the acre of diamonds within every personality.

In evaluating his years with people, Roy Burkhart said:

> "We can only understand man if we realize that he is a bundle of desires; his soul is characterized by its teachings. This pursuit is so basic to life that sensitive people do not know which is the greatest gift — finding truth or searching for it."

When God is in man, He makes man aware of his true destiny — that he was brought into the world for something more than he is now. Man is not himself yet, but he is related to God. It is God who lures man forward, who has placed the restlessness within and has given him hope to keep going.

Along with desire and discontent, two guides are essential. The first is to love God with the whole being — body, mind, strength, and soul. And the next is that man must love his neighbor as himself. Self-discovery bears with it the one insight and inspiration that can only be described as religion. Religion is one's personal relationship with God. Sin is your having your way with your life rather than letting God direct your life to its real purpose — its real personhood. If you are to reach the fulfillment of your inner dreams and deepest desires, if you are to find the inner resources you really want — God holds the way and the power for transformation.

There are many different ways of describing how men let God begin His inner transformation. Brother Lawrence, of the sixteenth century, told of the change coming to his life through seeing a leafless tree in winter. The thought occurred to him that if God could bless that dry stark tree to bring forth leaves, bloom, and fruit, that surely He could work a miracle in his life. This caused him to start on a quest with the belief that God could work a miracle in the heart. God will work the same miracle in your heart. The seed is already within you, let it grow through faith in God's love.

The quest for yourself grows in accordance to the acceptance of responsibility for the past, present, and future. Related to this is the willingness to identify with your own humanity.

Many people try to deny that they have primitive instincts and that they have any real destructive qualities. But these are prevalent and go on in their annihilating progress when they are not recognized.

Man has within him the nature of the most savage beast. Nowhere does he show this beastiality more than in the home among those who are nearest and dearest. Here he maims, wrecks, destroys, hurts, or lashes out in ways that have brought permanent damage and made havoc of his marriage. His frustrations often carried over from childhood cause him constant turmoil, upset, and defeat. He wants to be, but hasn't been. He starts out the day determined to be somebody and to do something worthwhile, but he returns to his house at the end of the day frustrated, disappointed, and defeated. No, so far he hasn't found the way but he can. Believe this — you can find the way.

You are responsible for knowing what you are, why you are, and when you will become different.

This is a responsibility that one cannot pass to someone else. Assistance can be given, but its final fulfillment must come to each person. This is done by checking the motives for everything that is done. The conscious mind will devise reasons for the things that are done which really have their genesis and explanation hidden in the unconscious. The unconscious mind controls nine-tenths of one's reactions and actions and the reason why; the conscious mind controls only one-tenth.

Each one must enable his conscious mind to explain those moments of intuition, those flashes of insight — why one can laboriously work on a problem all evening and go to bed without the solution, and then the next morning wake up and the answer to the problem comes to the mind like a flash. All experiences of the past have been stored in the unconscious mind; and, while one is sleeping, his unconscious mind goes on working with the problem and finally gives the conscious mind the answer. Dreams have done more to resolve man's dilemma than most realize. Each one must ask his conscious mind to explain the moments when he has strength and power greater than he believed he possessed. In the unconscious are stored emotional reserves and energies which come to the aid of the conscious life when desperate circumstances call for them.

"Man's extreme is God's opportunity" is the theological way of expressing a scientifically tested fact which stated psychologically would be: "Let one relax and open his mind to the truths that the unconscious can bring and the nervous system will bring it to reality."

It is the complete trust in God that makes for the righteousness which has been welling up in the inner being and lets it finish in its own way the work it has begun.

This is God's plan to open up to everyone what can be within his life. But each person has the responsibility of taking the initiative and seeing that he finds the proper help and that he sticks with it until his life begins to move more and more in the right direction that God would have it to be. "It is a sad day for everyone when he becomes absolutely content with the life he is living," admonished Phillips Brooks

"With the thoughts that he is thinking, with
   the deed he is doing,
When there is not forever beating at the
   doors of his soul some great desire
To do something larger which he knows he
   was meant to do
Because he is still, in spite of all, a
   child of God."

Man is also a victim of self-pity. If you are caught in self-pity and feeling sorry for yourself, this is the first place to start with yourself and change your self-image. Many people were surprised at the response Jackie Gleason made to a question about self-pity:

"I dislike pity in any form," he replied. "I think it's an excuse for cowardice. The great masochistic tranquilizer is self-pity. If you have a problem and try to figure it out — that's much more heroic than moaning and groaning and whining."

Every parent has the God-given opportunity to give children a right start in life. Religion is taught and caught in the home. Reality depends upon the daily evidence of God in the affairs of the home. Then it is up to the individual as to what life will be. For he alone chooses the way he will live and the way he will die. He can be thankful for home, church, school and community for a good start or see where these may have failed.

However, to blame someone else, circumstances, and wrong teachings for one's condition is not only dishonest, but it is an oversimplification of life. The problem is always within each person and is solved through the process of continuous awareness of God's presence, of self's limitations and strength, and of the determination to be authentic.

If it were as simple as some imply then all people would have to do is "kiss and make up" and everything would automatically fall in place. The bitterness, cynicism, complaining, littleness, and poor self-image that keeps so many from being authentic and real can be overcome. You must decide whether you want to be the victim or the victor.

There is a reason why you are like you are. But more important is the realization that there is a reason for being different. Christ came into the world so that you can be different — ". . . that you might have life and have it more abundantly."[1]

There is a reason to live — there is a reason why you don't have to stay as you are.

---

(1) John 10:10

CHAPTER XI

"THESE DAMN CONFLICTS"

Men must decide on what they will not do, and then they are able to act with vigor in what they ought to do.
— *Mencius*

The souls of men of undecided and feeble purpose are the graveyards of good intentions.
— *John Foster*

The man who has not learned to say "No" will be weak if not a wretched man as long as he lives.
— *A. Macloren*

"Chaplain, I don't know what in the world makes me have these damn conflicts," Tom Brown said. His face was flushed, he was angry, it seemed that he was about to explode. "It seems everytime I try to do anything right, I do it exactly wrong. I really don't want to do the things I do, and yet it seems there is some kind of compulsion always driving me away from it. For some reason or another, I've never seemed to feel at home with people. I try to go out with one crowd and drink with them; I go out with loose women and try to feel at home with them; then I try to get out with the other crowd, young people who go to church and those who try to do the right thing and yet I don't seem at home with them. One week I've tried to live their kind of life and the first thing I know, I'm out just raising hell in general. I just can't understand myself. I don't know what in the world makes me this way.

"I don't even feel at home with my own folks. I have a sister, younger brother, both my parents are living, yet it just seems that I don't fit in anywhere. What's wrong with me that I just can't seem to be at home with anybody?"

"Tell me something about your life as a child, Tom. Did both of your folks work and who reared you as a child?"

"Yes, both of my parents worked. The fact is that I can't ever remember being around my folks while I was a child. They always fussed at me. Mother and Daddy were always quarreling with each other. I usually was kept by somebody or stayed with my grandmother as a little child. After I started to school I can't ever remember coming home and finding my mother there. She worked in a mill and my father worked for a company and was out of town quite a bit. He did construction work. I can't remember any time in my life when either one of my parents told me they loved me. My mother has always been distant and aloof when the rest of the family and daddy sometimes tried to make us feel better by doing something for us, but he never did show us any affection. When he tried to show love toward us, it was buying us something or giving us something or taking us someplace. I know he must have had the best intentions, but I never have felt that my father or mother either one loved me."

"Did you feel lonely during those days as a child?"

"Yes, I always felt lonely. I don't know when I've ever felt at home with somebody or felt that somebody was with me. I never have really been able to feel close to anybody. I've tried to feed different girls my best line, tell them I loved them, that I thought a lot of them, but I can tell every girl the same thing and feel the same toward her. I never have felt really close to anybody and I never have felt like I really loved anybody. I've told many girls that I loved them and I've done everything in the book to make them think that I love them, yet I never have.

"And it just seems that whatever group I'm with I try to do something to get them to accept me. I've been living away from home while I'm working here at this place. I live with three other fellows in a house that we've rented. These other fellows are calloused; they just don't seem to care about anything and I've found myself doing anything and everything that they suggest just so I can be part of them. I'd just give anything if I could feel at home with them, if there were just somebody who just understood me; if there were just somebody who cared for me."

"Tom, have you ever gone with any girl or anyone whom you thought that you could feel close to or that you could love?"

"Yes, I did go with one girl who is just the kind of girl that I would really like to marry. When I'm around her I do feel better. I think she is the type of person I would like to be, yet no matter how hard I try, I just can't really express any genuine love to her. I have affection for her, I feel attracted to her, and yet I don't have any loyalty to her. I can be with her one night and talk to her and tell her how much I care for her, and then the next night be with someone else."

"Do you remember anything about your childhood and when you were around 3 or 4 years of age?"

"Not too much. I just remember as early as I can remember that I was lonely and felt that nobody cared for me. I know often times when I was 4 or 5 years of age that I would run away from home from the person that was keeping me, telling her that I wanted to find my mother, telling her that I wanted to see my mother, why wasn't my mother at home, why wasn't my mother keeping me? She would tell me my mother was doing what was best for me and trying to make a living for me, but that she couldn't be at home with me. I'd often tell her that I didn't care about my mama making a living for me, that I just wanted my mama home. I do know that I always thought that my mama and daddy didn't love me or they would be at home with me. I felt that they didn't love me because they never did show any affection to me. They never did show any love to me. They never did take me and put me in bed. They never did say prayers with me like some of the other children told me that their folks did. In fact, we never did have prayer when we ate our meals. Sometimes, when I've gone to visit some of my friends, they would ask the blessing at the meal. This never happened at our house. It just seems like there has never been any closeness in our family. I can't understand it. I don't know why I feel as I do.

"You ask me if I remember anything when I was 3 or 4 years old. It just seems like a very blank, dark period in my life. I know when I did anything wrong, that my folks fussed at me and that my daddy would give me a spanking when he got home. All I remember about those days was the scolding and the fussing at me that my mother did. I guess it must be something very wrong."

"Did your folks ever talk to you about sex in any way?"

"Yes, I remember when we would take baths or anything as children, my parents would never let any of us take baths together. And everytime we went to the bathroom, they would make us close the door so we would be by ourselves, and taught us that sex was kind of a nasty word for us, for us not to refer to any part of our bodies in any way. The word sex in our family has always been kind of a nasty word. I guess somehow or other I grew up to think that sex is something that maybe men want that women don't want, because I've often heard my father and mother talking in the night. She never did want to have any kind of sex relations with my father. I remember that as an early child. Why do you ask that? How could that affect my feelings on these things that I do?"

"It could fit into your life in many ways. I am asking you these questions and letting you tell me about your early life because the emotional patterns of any person are formed during the early years of your life. Everyone's emotional behavior is set by the time he is 12, and often they are formed by the time one is 7. And those ages between 3 and 5 are often the most important years of life. I would like for you to recall everything that you can during this particular period so that you can help me to understand you. Most of all this is also to help you to understand yourself, because as you go back and talk through these periods in your life, something will come to you that will help unravel a block that's been bothering you and you will begin to find your way through life. You see, as you go back and talk about these first 12 years of your life, you will discover something that someone has told you that you haven't quite dealt with emotionally and until you deal with it emotionally, you will not discover what is wrong with you. So, everything in these first 12 years can be resolved and looked into in such a way that you will be free from them. You have emotional bondage from these early years that in some way you have to be free from so that you can be your best self. This is why these things are important. This is one approach that has been very effective. Some counselors start where you are and get enough motion to begin overcoming the past."

As further conversation was held with Tom Brown from time to time, it was discovered that his parents had not shown love to him during those crucial years from 3 to 5 and because of this, he had never learned to love anybody. Love is a capacity that must be learned from someone else, and in order to love people, a person needs to receive love from someone. Tom had grown up without ever feeling at home or of being loved. Only through a process of several sessions with his chaplain and also in some group therapy with other people who began to show love for Tom did he begin to feel at home and find that which he had longed for so much in his life. The training in the home and in kindergartens is the most important to a child of 5. This is the age when a child begins to take on his consciousness of sex. His toilet training, the way a boy learns to identify with his mother through his daddy and the girl identifying with the daddy through the mother have a great part to do with emotional development.

Everyone has conflicts and compulsions. They vary in degree from what has happened in early childhood. Many parents give to their children the right kind of childhood and love which gives them a much better start than other children have, but everyone has some unhealthy emotions that they've picked up that have to be dealt with in some ways.

This has been proved in psychiatric counseling to the degree that one physician, Dr. Hugh Missildine, does all of his counseling on the basis of what he calls "your inner-child of the past" and whatever has happened in those early years. One can go back and use this as a guide to lead these people to health and to happiness within their emotional lives. Dr. Missildine has discovered that the behavior of parents toward the children in these early years will cause definite reactions and emotional conduct in the children that continue in adulthood.

He has shown that when the parents' attitude toward the child is excessive in perfectionism, that the affect on the adult will be an endless over-serious preoccupation with physical, intellectual or social accomplishment. When there has been excessive over-cohesion, an adult will spend a lot of time dawdling and daydreaming. Such a person will have a tendency toward procrastination and other forms of resistance. If there has been over-submission, the behavior will be impulsiveness, temper outbursts, lack of consideration for the rights of others. Where there has been over-indulgence, the consequences are boredom, lack of resistance, difficulty in initiating individual effort. When there has been too much emphasis placed upon the child as far as health is concerned, there has been anxiety about the health and providing an excuse for inactivity and nonparticipation as adults. Parents who have punished their children severely through life cause a fierce desire for revenge and often a very rebellious life. *When there has been neglect of the child, such as was experienced in Tom's life, there will be anxiety, loneliness, and difficulty in feeling close to others.* So often this type of person is unable to express any love and has to learn how to love. When there has been rejection, the adult will be a lone wolf and will feel that he does not accept himself. He often has real hatred for himself and is very destructive toward himself. If parents have been excessive in sexual stimulation of the children, the adult will have a tendency to put a great emphasis in the physical aspects of sex and dissatisfaction with personal relationships. The evidence that Dr. Missildine has given in his psychiatric work has been followed closely by many psychiatrists and counselors. They believe the approach to be very effective.

In Tom's case, by the constant assurance of other people of their love for him, he was able to overcome his feeling of being unaccepted, his feeling of loneliness, and his inability to love, and has been able to learn the capacity of love and how to get along with other people. The young lady, whom he wanted to love and to whom he had been attracted, was very emotionally mature. She was given knowledge of the basic problems Tom faced and became a participant in group therapy groups for further self-understanding. After two years, they were married. They continue to be in discussion groups to develop a better marriage. It takes from three to five years to get a marriage established on a strong foundation. A woman requires 17 years of married life to enter into her full womanhood. The man reaches his heights of sexual prowess at 19, while the woman does not reach the beginning of her deepest sexual capacities until she is 30. Love was not easy for Tom to receive. "Love is so painful," Tom often remarked. What he meant was that he had to go through the valleys of pain to be able to love and receive love.

Attitudes are so important in marriage and the understanding of the opposite sex is so important that any couple is wise to be in discussion groups, group therapy, other avenues of personality development, and emotional growth.

Since the desire to be loved, and to love and to have special value to some person, is the greatest desire of life, many people are frustrated because of this desire being unsatisfied. Another reason for the incapacity to love and receive love is considered in the next person who shares his feelings and circumstances.

Conflicts are caused by Ego, the conscious level of the human personality which makes the decisions and tries to maintain a balance in the conflicts of life. Id, the instinctive part of life, attempts to push Ego out into a field of battle where Id has his way. At the same time Super-Ego, the critical and tyrannical aspect of the personality, is saying Ego is making a mistake.

Dr. William C. Menninger and Munro Leaf give a picture that describes Id seeking to have his way in a group of pushing, energetic children waiting to get on the stage and strut their stuff. Id has these desires, compulsions, urges and impulses.

Ego is the stage doorkeeper and director of amateur night trying to keep everything in balance.

The audience is the outside world, and it is hard to please.

In the wings is the critic, Super-Ego, who can make Ego feel so depressed he will want to give up the show business.

Ego wants to go one direction and Id wants another. This brings into being what is called defense mechanism which attempts to bring behavior that satisfies both.

A highschool boy may fear to participate in a football game, but rather than admit the fear he compensates by saying he is ill, his back hurts, or he has a sprained ankle. Fear can stir up an unconscious conflict that causes a paralysis of the arm or leg.

Different kinds of defense mechanism take place in normal behavior, but they need to be understood. They vary as Compensation, Rationalization, Idealization, Reaction, Formation, and Displacement.[1] Any of these can be used to an extreme and rob an individual of a satisfactory life.

Compensation is a natural thing when a blind person develops a more sensitive touch. One may become an expert in some field of human endeavor because of inabilities in another. A highschool

---

[1] William C. Menninger and Munro Leaf, *You and Psychiatry,* New York, Charles Scribner's Sons, 1948, pp 113-123

boy unable to participate in athletics memorized the baseball standings of athletes and became an expert of information.

Rationalization is the personality's explanation of feelings, ideas, behavior as coming from some other source than his Id (instincts). Anyone thinking fate, luck, or bad breaks are the reason for his misfortune is fooling himself by rationalization.

Idealization can be funny in its mild form but can be very objectionable when used in an extreme form. The wife or husband describing a mate as the most beautiful, considerate, and sweetest is acceptable, but any individual who thinks he is flawless is obnoxious. Everyone has a tendency to overlook faults in himself that he sees so quickly in others.

Everyone wants to look good before his friends. The roads to this goal are self-confidence, self-assurance, and a reasonable faith in one's intelligence.

Reaction Formation is seen in the slips of speech. One may plan to express a compliment. Instead he says what he feels. A woman thinks a hat is unattractive. She exclaims, "What a perfectly ugly hat," when she wanted to describe, "What a perfectly beautiful hat."

Displacement is the process by which the emotional value attached to one idea or person is transferred to another idea or person. When man displaces his positive feelings of love, it is a good mechanism. If he displaces his negative ones of hate to other people, it is a bad mechanism.

Parents and teachers who have so much contact with children while they are forming life patterns would be wise to evaluate their own emotional demonstrations to be sure they don't make the wrong displacements.

CHAPTER XII

CAN I EVER LIVE AGAIN?

Death and love are the two wings that bear the good man to Heaven.
— *Michelangelo*

Be still prepared for death; and death or life shall thereby be sweeter.
— *Shakespeare*

The gods conceal from men the happiness of death, that they may endure life.
— *Lucan*

Mildred Emerson asked this question. "Can I ever live again? Since Larry died my whole world seems gone. There were just the two of us and we had been married such a short time. Seems that we had just begun to live. We had been married only five years and our marriage had become so beautiful and now he's gone." These words were expressed when sympathy was offered in the home and she was still under the first part of the shock of grief. Grief has three aspects – it has that period of unreality where it seems that it cannot be true that a loved one has died. When death does become real and the reality of it dawns on a person, then the bereaved goes through a period of recoil which normally lasts only a period of a few weeks. But, if grief is not dealt with properly, it can go on and on and lead to much bitter resentment and hatred. And then there comes the third stage – which is rehabilitation. When Mildred began to talk more, she had gone through the stage of unreality and had begun to come to the office to resume her work and talk through her feelings. It was very important that the chaplain had seen her in the first hour of her grief. This enabled him to identify with her through each stage of her sorrow and pain.

"It seems so unfair that God would let Larry die when we were just beginning to live. I just have to admit that I resent God, that I hate Him for letting my husband die. Here we were, just at the beginning of life and everything was going our way. We had a new home, he was making good in his business, he had already been made a Junior Executive in the company, we had a new car, a beautiful set of furniture, a television, and it just seemed like we had everything to make life go. I just can't understand how God could do me this way. I really don't have any reason for living. I just don't see how I can go on. I don't know what I'm going to do about it but I've just about decided that it's just not worth trying, and that I'm just going to give up. I don't care about being around any of our old friends. Everything they say to me just sounds silly and ridiculous. They don't understand. They try to give me pep talks. I want to go home and just get away from it all. It's a real pain to come down here to work. Wherever people are and whatever they try to say just doesn't make any sense to me. I really just feel like I'm going crazy because no matter what I feel nor what I say – life's just never the same."

"Mildred, life will never be the same for you. I do know how you feel and want to be with you as a friend to help. It just never will be – whatever you do, you'll have to learn to live with realization that things will not be like they were. It's up to you whether you're going to want to live. Right now you feel as though you're the only one who has ever gone through anything like this — that God has picked you out to treat you unjustly. The first part of reality is to know that this has happened to many others."

"I guess that part of it is right, it just seems that I'm often in some kind of dream world. I just find myself going around in circles and my head swimming all the time. There is a tightness in my throat all the time and it just seems that I'm going to suffocate. It's hard for me to breathe without drawing deep breaths and I've got a numbness and hollowness in my stomach. My mouth is dry and every time I try to eat anything, it's just like sawdust. I don't feel good and it just seems that I can't think and can't react to anything. I'm tired all the time. I just can't sleep or rest regardless of how many drugs the doctor gives me to make me sleep. I'm tired all the time. I just don't feel like doing anything and it just seems that I'm not able to pick up my feet. They're so heavy and my legs feel like they weigh a ton. I just have to make myself get up and walk — even to walk across the room.

"Everything seems so empty inside me. I'm just empty. Life is drab. It's dark. It's dull. And I just feel terrible. I don't feel like anybody loves me. I don't feel like anybody cares for me. I don't feel like there is any reason to live. I just don't feel like I can do anything. Some people have written me letters to try to help me out but I don't even appreciate them. I don't appreciate anything that anybody has been trying to do for me. I know this sounds unreasonable. I know I'm being unreasonable. This is just the way I feel. I don't think I can change my feelings. I just feel that I'm a machine running without any control from me at all."

"Mildred, you're describing the way everyone feels in the time of deep grief and the best thing about this whole thing is that you're able to talk about how you really feel and be able to describe it. There is a book that is given by this company to people in the time of grief that I want you to read, called *Grief's Slow Wisdom*[1] and these are the normal patterns of grief. When you read this, you will see that it's describing exactly what you've been saying today."

"Is it a normal thing for me to be feeling that Larry is right along with me? I dream about him. I have visions about him. I find myself talking to him. And one thing that has been helpful — it seems like in these visions and dreams that everything

[1] Cort R. Flint, *Grief's Slow Wisdom*, published by Droke House Publishers, Anderson, South Carolina.

is all right for him and that he's happy where he is."

"Mildred, there is no real explanation how these things take place, but they do take place and many people have experienced what you're talking about. You have told me before you came for these conferences, that you and Larry were quite active in your church and that you're religious people. Religious people do have sometimes a deeper sense of a loved one being with them after death than other people do. As we talk through things, we will have to deal with your feelings as to how you really feel and we'll just have to find a way."

"Sometimes, you know, I feel guilty as though there is maybe something that I have done or something I didn't do that could have brought happiness to Larry or something that I've done to cause this death."

"This is one of the things we need to work on — separating any sense of guilt away from your grief. Your grief is rough enough without you trying to make it worse by imposing guilt on yourself. However, you need to talk out your feelings of guilt now in such full descriptions that you can decide whether there is guilt or whether it is a period of grief that will disappear. No one is perfect, but you have told me of the beautiful love shared by Larry and you. When you have experienced deep love it will come through for you now."

There is no more devastating experience than the deep grief that comes from the death of someone very near and dear. Mildred has given only a portion of her feelings to encourage someone to receive further help by talking with a competent pastor or other counselor.

Grief is love. Those who love deeply will grieve deeply. For grief to be resolved, one must face up to the reality that the departed has gone, never to return to this earth. The grief is there and it must be recognized. It cannot be buried without bringing drastic consequences that no one can afford to have.

There are three reasons for grief. First, is the grief for self and sadness that one is deprived of his loved one. This one is not present to bring companionship, joy and strength. In a certain sense, such grief is homesickness for the departed. One must see that there is much selfishness about death in that self becomes the main concern. This is a very natural consequence of death.

Second, there is fear. Suddenly, the world has changed and the future is so uncertain as to what to do and what is going to happen. Many old fears begin to show their faces again and the individual reverts back to another emotional age when he felt inadequate and afraid.

Third, there is insecurity. All seems to be lost and for a while hope is gone.

Because of the deep effects on the physical body as well as the spiritual and emotional sides, one should seek immediate guidance in grief.

Mildred accepted the fact that life would never be the same, but she believed she had a purpose in life. This purpose would be different, but she decided to live at her highest and best as though she was on a journey and would be returning to Larry. This helped her in the first year after his death to have a will to a meaningful life. There were many days she thought she wouldn't make it, but she learned to live one day at a time and deal with her depression and inspirations on this basis.

TRUTHS FOR COMFORT*

1. Death brings some of the deepest grief and the darkest hours of life. There is no way one can be fully prepared for it.

2. You can win the battle with grief. You can win for your own benefit, for the sake of loved ones, and for the fulfillment of God's continued purpose in your life.

3. One of the hallmarks of Christian mental and emotional maturity is the recognition and acceptance of the certainty of death.

4. "We understand death for the first time when he his hand upon one whom we love" — Madame de Stael.

5. If you are to resolve your grief, you must face up to its reality and then talk about it to someone who is competent to share your grief with you.

6. Grief is love.

7. Each one who has experienced grief must reach up and receive the outstretched hand of God, and in His presence find the help that wins the victory.

*Cort R. Flint, *Grief's Slow Wisdom*, Droke House Publishers.

CHAPTER XIII

"IS THERE A PILL?"

Life is a long lesson in humility.
— *James M. Barice*

He lives long that lives well; and time misspent is not lived, but lost.
— *Fuller*

Life, like waters of the sea, freshens only when it ascends toward Heaven.
— *Richter*

"Is there a pill that you can take to control you from doing something that is ruining your life and your husband? I know something has to be done. I thought by your working with people in their problems that you could tell me which doctor to go to and get the right capsule for healing me."

The chaplain thought at first she was joking, but then he realized she was intensely serious. "No, there is no way to find peace in a capsule. A pill can't do it. When we have problems, we are the pills. We have to be turned inside out so that we can get rid of our unhealthy emotions and pick up the healthy ones. We have to understand ourselves and why we do what we do before we are conscious of the compulsions that drive us to these things that bring depression and despair."

Jane Parsons had all of the markings of a very distinguished woman. She was beautiful, brown hair with brown eyes, about 5 feet 4 inches. Her figure showed discipline. She kept herself neat and well dressed. Her bearing was confident. She was radiant and most people would have thought of her as the one person who really didn't have any problems. She came to share her particular needs because her husband was associated with a business that carried on a very close relationship to the one where the chaplain was working full time. As she began to talk, her countenance changed. She lost all appearances of confidence and tears began to flow. She laid her head down on the desk and wept for about ten minutes before she could even begin to say anything.

"I don't know where to begin, I'm just messed up in every way. I'm about to ruin my husband's chance for any kind of promotion within his company — even to continue with the company. I don't know why I do it, but there's just something in me that has to go out and get on a binge, not with alcohol as many do, but a buying spree. I have closets full of clothing but I just have to go out and buy more clothes, jewelry, hand bags, shoes, trinkets, and any other kind of ornament, expensive perfumes, or just anything that makes me stand out and get noticed. These rings I'm wearing are far beyond what anybody should have invested in rings. Just think of having a diamond that costs $25,000.00, but I had to have one. Somebody else had one so I had to have one. I've just about ruined my husband's credit. We are just barely able to keep our head above water because of the sprees that I have. I know it must be similar to what an alcoholic has."

"Tell me some of the personal memories of your childhood and let's see how everything fits in place about what you're facing."

"My earliest memories were of the poverty in our family and our being cold, going barefooted to school when other kids had shoes. There were ten children in our family and I was right in the middle. There were five boys and five girls. The older members of the family always pushed off on me the things they were supposed to do and then I found myself taking care of the younger ones most of the time. I really had compassion for them, but always resented the fact that the family pushed off so much on me. My father was the strict disciplinarian of the family and never gave us a chance to explain why we did something. He whipped us when he thought we had fallen short, and this was something that we faced all the time. All the other kids at school would talk about me and call me names — even names like Raggedy Ann and that girl who thinks she's something, but she's nothing. I remember walking through the swamp lands, having my feet in the mud, as a child everything about life just seems kinda smutty, muddy, dreary, and we were so poor. I swore to myself that sometime I was going to have something, and that I wasn't going to always be poor. I just hated life as it was. I don't even like to think about it. I guess one reason that I haven't had any children is the fact that I just don't want to be responsible for a bunch of brats running around the house like we had. You talk about my early life — it was miserable. Something I think of as cold, gray, dark. The only happy moments we had was when someone gave us something and we had some clothes to wear that had been handed down by someone else or special times such as Christmas and Thanksgiving when we did have turkey and other food that was given to us by some of the people of the community. My father and mother both worked. They just seemed to never get a job that paid enough where we could have the things that we needed. Our house was always cold and never could keep the windows in it. We would put oil-skin paper or something in to fill in the cracks. Due to so many children, it just seemed that we never could do anything. My father was a tenant farmer, my mother helped him with the farm and my daddy did some work for the neighbors. But, it just seemed like we always had tough breaks. I never felt close to anybody and I don't feel close to anybody today. I guess my life has always been filled with resentment toward people, and I've always had a certain hostility about life as it is. And I married Larry because I needed to get into a good home and he could make a good living. I guess I haven't been the wife to him that I ought to have been. I don't know what's wrong with me and don't know what's made me act like I have. I know I resented my daddy's harshness and resented being born into a family that was so poor, and I know I should love my family and be grateful for them. But, when I get around them it just reminds me of poverty. I find myself every time Larry leaves home, getting panicky, feeling insecure, and the only thing that satisfies me and takes me out of my depression is to go on one of the binges and buy these things. Since Larry's in the sales department of his company, he is away a good deal of time. Even though our house has everything about it that is different, at times I feel that old cold dampness closing in on me and that mud coming through my toes — being slimy. And I just don't know what to do so I just go out and buy these things. Then I'm also of the idea that I desperately need to keep up with everybody else."

"Mrs. Parsons, one of the things that would help right now is to stop and realize that one of the deepest things about a woman and one of her greatest desires to be secure. There is a sense in which you have been looking for some kind of security all of your life and these things to some degree have been your attempt to get things to bring this security. See a woman has a little mask about her, that as long as she has everything alright within this little circle she feels alright, but when something happens to upset that little circle she begins to feel insecure and has to find the real inner resources of life that bring security."

"You mean I'm trying to satisfy my life with things when what I really need is something within myself that I have a sort-of false security."

"Yes, life needs to be built on inner resources and you don't find these within things. They have to come from within yourself. I would like for you to go ahead and tell me more things that you remember from your childhood."

"There are lots of things that I don't like to tell. They don't sound very good. I guess I've got to bear my heart to somebody, and I trust you and know that you won't let me down. But, you know I did many things while I was in high school to be accepted in the crowd. I was always envious of the girls whose folks had everything. The crowd that I so envied... so I decided I'd pay any price to be a part of it since sex relations was an accepted thing, drinking, certain amount of drugs, and I began to participate in all of that. I'll never forget when I first gave myself to a boy. He was captain of the football team and every girl wanted to go with him. He made me believe that if I came across and made out with him that I was going to be the girl in his life. This was great for about six months and then he dropped me and I felt like I'd been kicked out in the back alley so then I just didn't care. This kind of life continued in that I did begin to have affairs with several boys, but I got to stay in the group. Now, I realize it was a price that I would never want to pay again. I realize that it was a mistake."

"You're at about rock bottom, nothing much to lose by having a little faith. The main thing to remember about the past is to realize as you talk it out and resolve your emotions you can begin an entirely new life. Think how wonderful it is that there is a God who will forgive you, blot out the past, and make life what it really needs to be."

"You know, I've never talked with anybody about this and it feels good just getting it out in the open where I can look at it. It makes me look like trash. I know it does. That's what I was and now I've gone off on something like this seemingly just as bad and going to be just as damaging to my husband."

"Since you mentioned some of these things that could have some deep implications, I would like for you to talk with this psychiatrist friend of mine that has a religious outlook and one that you can take in confidence. He works with us when we ask for cooperation. I think that possibly you would want to talk with him some too."

"I'm willing to do anything to get this thing squared away and straightened out."

Jane had some conferences with the psychiatrist and also took part in some group therapy and this way she did find out some of the difficulties that she had to face.... some of the emotional barriers that were between her and emotional health. She found that some of the reactions she had were the same that many people make to overcome poverty and fulfill this desire to be accepted. When her husband, Larry, was brought in on the conferences he was very sympathetic. He had previous training in human relations groups and other forms of understanding that made him very desirous to help his wife. This is always a very important phase of the home because it takes two to make a marriage. They both were able to realize some of the weaknesses and the strength of each other and began to give support to each other.

After a couple of years of this type of counseling, Jane was asked what it was that had helped her most to find her way.

"I think that the first thing that helped me was to realize that there was someone who understood me, accepted me as I was, what I'd been, and did not look down his nose at me. For some reason, I'd always felt that religious people would look down their nose to anybody who had lived the kind of life I had or had any problems. I didn't realize that there were genuine people in the church who were like a doctor when someone had broken an arm and that these people feel their job is to be a hospital for sinners rather than a hotel for saints. I think this is one of the big helps that started me on the road to recovery.

"Second, I came to recognize that reality and unreality have a great gap between them. All of my life, I had been living in a dream world — trying to make things appear different from what they were rather than facing up to reality as to what life was and how I could find inner strength for it.

"Third, religious faith came to be very meaningful in my life. I did make a commitment of my life to God. I confessed my sins to him and found a beginning within my life that made possible my having a new center. Then it was that these inner resources began to develop in my life.

"Fourth, was when I realized that the deepest drive in life is self survival — self preservation. Then I could see why I had been so selfish about some things. I'd never heard anybody say before that self preservation was the strongest drive in a person. Self understanding was the way that I began to be able to work with myself, and as you sometimes stated — be a good parent to myself. I realized that I had the responsibility for myself and I must do something myself. Then the idea that sex was the next strongest drive in me — I could see why that many of my problems took form in my sex life and also about this desire for security that I was trying to get the insecurity satisfied by things. But, only as I began to be real and quit being a phony that I had any meaning for my life and security within my life.

"There are many things that I could say that were helpful but probably this was what helped me most."

Security is one of the foundations upon which mental and emotional health rests. This is not a matter of what is possessed in money, food, clothing, or the kind of a home owned. It is an intangible that has no pat methods and answers.

There are two basic securities needed for man's well being. The first is the inner harmony and peace that resolve the tensions in all the selves. No external environment can give security without the inside balance.

A second basic need is to be loved, to love, and to have a unique meaning to someone. A man experiencing genuine love is secure. The person now receiving the deep love of another has come to a mature relationship where he is getting a great dividend in the investment he has made in others.

The most unfortunate are those who want to love others and make friends but do have the capacity for love and do not know how to give or accept love. Some experience has taken place and caused them to resist all love. They build cages around themselves and obstacles to every door that might open to them.

Security comes by right handling of environment in relationship to inner peace.

THOUGHTS FOR CONSIDERATION

1. There are patterns of behavior which are positive. They help solve a crisis.

2. Negative behavior and thinking worsen the situation and weaken any person for his future.

3. To the extent an individual faces the reality of his situation and actively wrestles with it, the stronger he emerges.

4. To the extent that another person flees from the realities, he sets the stage for a worsened pattern of adjustment to life.

5. There are three R's to healing in the human personality. They are Reality, Responsibility, and Right Behavior.

6. One must not crumple when he feels he is not bearing up as strongly as someone else might. None can afford to criticize himself and cut his foundation for life and health.

7. Reacting to a crisis by positive action has a double benefit. In this way one can be actively contributing to the solution of his crisis and also he takes his mind off his troubles.

CHAPTER XIV

"UNDERSTANDING YOUR DREAMS"

Nothing so much convinces me of the boundlessness of the human mind as its operation in dreaming.
— *Chulow*

We are somewhat more than ourselves in our sleep, and the slumber of the body seems to be but the working of the soul.
— *Sir T. Browne*

Psychologists say that the chief frustration of this day is hostility. It might be surprising to learn how much hostility can build up in a person so that even a total stranger might kick off the valve that lets the steam out.

"Men! men! men! I hate their guts. Don't try to talk to me about men. I hate every damn one of them!"

This was the opening statement of a very beautiful blonde sitting behind the desk as the chaplain walked into her office. She was a junior executive of a very fine organization.

Everywhere you go people are angry and if pushed enough in any direction are able to let go. Anger is one of the four basic patterns of behavior instincts or emotions whichever the definition that a person might want to select. Anger is more than any one of these and yet is all of them. Everyone gets mad and it is good to recognize it. It is what is done with the anger and how it is gotten out of the system that enables a person to have emotional health. Dreams can reveal the source of hostility if the dreams are understood.

But, let us listen to Lucille James' story.

The chaplain replied to her stormy outburst, "I don't believe I said anything about men....I'm just visiting here in the offices and wanted to make your acquaintance."

"I heard that you were coming...I suppose you are going to hand out some of those pious platitudes that most chaplains and ministers have to say to people. I want you to know they don't mean a thing to me and I don't care to hear any of them!"

"I hadn't planned to hand out any platitudes, but I am interested in what you think platitudes are," was the chaplain's reply.

"To me its just a lot of religious nonsense that makes me want to puke. I've heard it from the pulpit, I've heard it from people talking, and I've seen it in people – that you're not supposed to do this; you're not supposed to do that; you're not supposed to live this way and life just isn't that way. It's nothing but heartache and turmoil."

"What made you say that you hated men so much? What did I do that provoked this out of you?"

"You didn't do anything to provoke it out of me. I just saw you as another man and a preacher and I'm fed up with both."

"Tell me about these men that have caused such damage to your life."

"What do you care about how I feel? What difference does it

143

make to you? Nobody really cares about anybody else in this world. It is hate – hate – hate, fight – fight – fight, get him before he gets you. Women and men have the same attitude; everybody is bringing confusion and turmoil to each other."

"Tell me about the men that have made you feel this way."

"Well, I'll tell you – not that I think that you care, but this is a day that I need to get something out of my system so it might as well be you as anybody else. I got married when I was nineteen. Married a man who was twenty-one and was in the Navy. He was reared in a home where he had everything he wanted and never has known anything about how to make a living. It seemed that every time he came home there was a big fuss and we stayed together just long enough to get me pregnant and have another child over a period of seven years. Then one day he just walked out and that was it. I don't know as I feel bad that he walked out because we didn't have anything in our home. We got a divorce but you know that we just never have had a moment of satisfaction or peace. I always heard that marriages were made in heaven but mine must have been made in hell because it was a hell of a mess from beginning to end. My husband never assumed any responsibility. I always had to make the living. Whatever money he got from the Navy, he squandered on himself on whatever he wanted to do. He's gone through with everything that his family left him and I've had to make a living for myself and the children ever since."

"As soon as I became a divorcee, everywhere I went a man offered to help me in my loneliness and to be sure that I wasn't missing anything in my sex life. I thanked them for their interest but to me, all they were doing was expressing their passions like an animal. To me sex is just like an animal. The way most people think about it and the way they live."

"What makes you feel that sex is just like an animal?"

"My first introduction to sex was when someone took me out to the riding stables. The person was a man about thirty-five years old and I was only sixteen. As we went out to the stables there were the stallion and the mare together and he laughed as the stallion was breeding the mare, but to me it made me sick and later on that same day he tried to rape me while we were out riding the horses. Every time a man approaches me now, I feel that same nausea and same repulsiveness that I felt when I was watching the stallion and the mare and the same feeling I had when this man, who was supposed to be a friend of our family, tried to rape me. I recognize that every divorcee is going to find this wherever she is and that where you work there are going to be people who feel this way, but I certainly did not expect it from the husbands of my best friends — this is certainly an animal world."

"Did you get married again?"

"Yes, I got married again to a man that I thought was deeply religious. A man that told me he thought God was leading us together. He was a lay preacher in his particular denomination. He took me around to a lot of the conventions — I was thrown in religious circles, and there was nothing wrong with him. Only he had been overly protected by his mother and some way or the other just had never grown up as a man. He couldn't enter into normal sex relations and this made me feel filthy and vile just like a worm or something. Every time I was around him, I felt something just creeping over me — like insects crawling over my skin — biting on me. I wanted to be needed. I wanted to fill a place in his life. I wanted us to have a happy home but it was everything else but that again. I hate men because everything that I've ever had in relationship to them has been so disappointing and has come so far short of what it ought to be."

"There is something that you might ought to give consideration to and that is that when you hate, you're paying the price for what other people have done. In the language of the church it might be called 'paying the price of the sins of other people', or whatever language you want to use. You're making yourself suffer for what other people have done. I'm not blaming you for your attitude, but I'm saying that you're working against yourself is what you're doing at this present time."

"I guess you're going to tell me that I'm supposed to feel a certain way. I'm not supposed to hate. I'm not supposed to do this or that. I've heard all that psych stuff that I want to hear."

"No, I'm not telling you that you're not supposed to feel any certain way. I'm trying to talk about how you do feel and possibly as you talk about how you feel you might find that you do not want to continue feeling that way about it. It's not how you're supposed to be, but it's how you are that we're dealing with. You do feel this way, but you can choose whether you want to continue to feel this way. It seems to be bringing unhappiness and if it's bringing unhappiness — why would you want to hold on to it? You're saying you have a right to get even with them — aren't you?"

"Yes, I'm saying I have a right to get even with them."

"How are you getting even with them? Someone wrote that hate is like burning down a barn to kill a rat, but the barn is your building — burning down is your own life. Do you want to destroy your own life to get the rats?"

"I hadn't thought about it that way. I am really unhappy and I would like to have a different kind of life. I don't know where to go or how to go. You seem to have a little better understanding of what I'm facing. Maybe there is a God that's interested in somebody like me."

"Yes, there is a God that's interested in someone like you and even though neither of us may have realized it when we first met — God has made it possible for us to meet so that healing might come to your life. There is a love of God that flows through people that brings healing and He wants all of us to be healed by this love. This is one of the purposes of love is to be healed. The experiences that you've been through make it very difficult for you to let love flow through. Our human nature always has that tendency to hate, to resent, and we're born with that, but we're not born with the capacity to love. This is something that has to be learned."

After three or four conferences with this young lady, the next conference started off by her saying that "I'm very grateful for what you've done for me. I have begun to see life differently, but perhaps its because I'm still so young in this new dimension of life that I have many deep and serious doubts and need reassurance that this life is real. When I'm away from the stimulus of your thoughts, questions, and conversations, I always feel a tendency to withdraw to get back into that other world in which I used to live. It's just that I haven't had the luxury of this miracle of communication on heart-to-heart level and when I'm away I begin to have doubts. But, I have begun to see and comprehend so much more to my life. I'm not afraid of God. How can you be afraid of God when He is so good and kind. When He seeks to do so much.

"I must admit that I had doubts about you as I began to talk about myself. I've been trying to find someone that understood me for so long that it has been difficult to really pour out my life. I ask can I trust you? Can I ask you questions that really trouble me and bother me? Will you understand that I'm not asking these in an ordinary way? Now that I have crossed over the three dimensional life of physical being, emotional being, and intellectual being, I am really enjoying this fourth dimension of a spiritual being. I am a new person with a new center in my life, but I realize that I have so much more to be worked out in me. I really don't care about the three dimensions, but am well aware of their existence and influence. I know that I must surely learn to deal with them before I can proceed to do anything else. It's so rare, so precious, so meaningful to be given somebody that recognizes the three dimensions of life but can move from them into the fourth dimension. A whole new broad exciting vista has been opened to me. There are no limits. Is there a limit to God? Are we not meeting His image? Is the only limit our physical body? Is death freedom from this restriction? We must be like a rocket waiting, getting ready, being built for the time of our release – our blast off. The closing of my eyes in death is all that it takes – yet I know that I must be ready to live before I die. Surely in God's wisdom there must be a time for this.

"In two of our talks before, I mentioned to you about the death of my father. It was such a relief to find somebody who understood that when you love someone dearly that you're going to have deep grief. No one had ever told me that before and this has been a big help to me. I realize now that my dad knew and understood so much about life. He is only a blink of the eye away. Sure I want him back. I need him, but since I can't have him return, why should or why would I rob him of his glory. Even though I know he would re-enter this physical cage if it was necessary, he loves me that much, but it isn't necessary and I wouldn't ask it of him. Christ did this for us and it's really quite adequate. It's all we need to know, isn't it? We can't quite get hold of reality can we? In one of our conversations and dialogues you said something about the love of God is ultimate reality. I believe that now. It is through His love that I have come to reality and realized that the world I was living in just wasn't real."

The next conference, the conversation began this way. "You know you compared this new life to coming into the water and that being in the water was fine, to jump in... it was when I did this that I joined the human race and began to be myself. I liked the book *To Thine Own Self Be True* by Dr. Flint. It is in beginning to be my real self facing reality that life is beginning to pour into this dead carcass of mine. Somehow, the words splash, and seem to run through my mind and I go back to some of my old stuff that I first said that it's not supposed to be like that but *it is – it is – it is.* There's just so much silly old sunshine bubbling around in life like this. One of these days my friends are going to be accusing me of taking LSD; however, it is not all typical sunshine is it? There are most unusual strange things too — I'm not questioning. Perhaps I can best describe it by using the term floating... floating and feeling the water that I have taken for granted heretofore. That is why this book *To Thine Own Self Be True*[1] helped me so much. It just kept bringing the words before me that helped me to see that no one can have a meaningful life until he is himself. I like the closing statement on the back of the book that 'this is life's greatest opportunity and man's highest privilege.' I realize now that this is my greatest opportunity and highest privilege — to be myself.

"One of the things that you told me was to remember my dreams. My dreams have played a large part in helping me with things. You also mentioned that when I had some of my high moments to recall some of these deadly things of the past that I hadn't resolved and it would help me to move on through them, as well as bringing some of the inspiration and joys for a better life. The other night I woke up from a dream with my heart pounding. I was in a house and suddenly it seemed to dawn on me that there were kittens somewhere in the house. I saw the mother cat and realized that I hadn't seen her for sometime and there must be kittens — but where. It also seemed that the children were hiding the kittens because they were afraid that I wouldn't let them keep them. I found them in a room that I didn't know was there or perhaps a room that I hadn't been in for a long time. I opened the door and there they were — mess all over the floor; what looked like blood, but the kittens were horrible... hairless... bloated stomachs. So repulsive that I picked one up and in anger yelled my first husband's name and that's when I woke up.

"I know what the cats are and I think I know that my first husband and my marriage to him holds the key to my withdrawal. I feel that I must empty these things out of my life that I know that I will never bury them again in myself. I don't want to look at these nasty cats, but I don't want them in my house either."

It was through a deeper understanding of her dreams that this young lady gave a lot of insight into her life and what to do about it.

HOW DREAMS HELP OUT

Dreams play an important role in the development of the human

---

[1] Cort R. Flint, *To Thine Own Self Be True*, published by Droke House Publishers, Anderson, South Carolina

personality. Most dream analysts take the position that some actions, characters, and settings are important while others are not. The determining factor is what the analyst has learned about the waking life of the person being analyzed.

Anything that forces someone to think about himself will help gain insights into what motivates him and makes him tick. Socrates' admonition "to know thyself" is sound advice. Attempting to gain insight through dreams is one way to contribute to self-knowledge.

Often people remark that they do not dream. Scientific research has proved that everybody dreams several times through the night.

Dr. Eugene Aserinsky, a research assistant at the University of Chicago, began the first scientific studies of the physiology of dreaming in 1953. While studying the sleep habits of newborn babies, he noticed at regular intervals the eyes of sleeping babies would move very rapidly behind the babies' closed eyelids. Sometimes these periods of rapid eye movement would be as brief as ten minutes. Then, at other times, they would last as long as half an hour.

Dr. Aserinsky would then attache electro encephalographs...machines which measure brain-wave patterns...to the infant's heads. He discovered during this period there was a similarity in the brain to wave patterns of infants who were awake. He theorized that they were dreaming. After testing adults he found this same rapid-eye-movement accompanied their dreaming. Other scientists have come to this same conclusion.

If a person is interested in seeing the insight that dreams give, he should begin to keep a diary of his dreams and discuss them with someone specializing in this field of study. The more writing of the dreams will bring some self-knowledge and thereby is worthwhile.

Russell Moore had some very deep things in his life that were difficult for him to understand. He was executive vice-president of a large chain of banks and was successful in every way that men would consider success. He was still very young, only forty-two years of age, yet there was something in him that made it impossible for him to be satisfied with himself. There was an unknown quality that was mystifying.... he did not understand himself. As he sought help, it was suggested that he remember his dreams. The counsellor was a specialist in dreams and their meaning. As Russell and the counsellor began research into his dreams, certain ones were repeated. One dream occurred over and over in which he was a doctor ministering to people no other

149

doctors would tend. In one dream he went to a home, where there were lots of children. As he moved among these children, they were telling him how much they loved him. The parents also told him of their appreciation of him and these words filled him with a warm glow. After many visits to this family, he was successful in restoring health to the ill members and enabling the whole family to find a happy and good life.

In another recurring dream he was a minister of a church. In this church, which had a large, spacious sanctuary, the attendance was very small. But as news of his sermons spread through the community the crowds became larger. Again, as in the former dream, the people began telling him how much they cared for him what a change he made in their lives. In one dream, of this pattern, he was helping a man who had had difficulty finding a job. In another, he was helping a woman who had been discarded by society.

After several sessions, the counsellor started asking Russell questions about his childhood. A probing into his early years brought out the fact that he had had great difficulty in feeling that he was accepted. He did things that would endear him to people. He sought for people to accept him in the role he was playing... thinking that if they did this, they would soon accept him for himself. In all of his dreams, he was in the role of one who was helping others and being acclaimed for his good deeds.

The analyst was able to show him that his feeling of not being accepted was a basic problem and as they talked, over a period of time, he was able to find the solution to his problem.

There are many people, like Russell, who feel rejected in their youth and, when these emotions are not resolved, these feelings are carried over into their adulthood.

James Winters was a leading physician in his community and was often included in the parties that the chaplain attended. At one of these affairs, the two men engaged in conversation. The doctor remarked to the chaplain, "You know, Chaplain, I would give anything if I could feel I was helping people like you are. I mend their bodies, prescribe medicines, and get them going for a while, but you are doing something for them that lasts for eternity." A little later in the conversation, the doctor told the chaplain of a dream that he had over and over. In this dream he was a pig who ran from place to place trying to find a home, but nobody would have him.

The reason for the recurring dream was his deeply-rooted feeling that nobody loved or cared for him. His low opinion of himself caused him to dream of himself as a pig. He had never married and this added to his feeling that no one could love him.

Another dream the doctor had concerned a train that he was to take a trip on. But, as the train was preparing to leave, a fog or haze would settle around it which prevented the journey.

As this dream was studied, it seemed to show his desire to get away from the situation he was in and the fog was a reminder that there was nothing he could do to remove himself from a seemingly impossible situation.

He, also had a dream about a dog which was traveling with him. The dog would run into the road and he would have to rescue the animal from danger. It might be a car or a horse being ridden down the road or someone maliciously hurting the dog. The dream suggested the doctor feared that he could never enjoy companionship or affection because of incidents in his childhood.

Through the study of his dreams, with the counsellor, he gained insight into his fears and basic problems and could begin the positive therapy which helped him overcome them.

Dreams are often used as a means of enabling people do things they would otherwise not do in working out their feelings.

John Waters was afraid to stand in front of a group and speak. Yet, he was in work where it was constantly necessary for him to be before people. He took courses in public speaking and motivation. In his dreams, he stood before people and spoke with ease. As this dream was repeated he found that in his waking life he could be at ease more and more. The realization of his acceptance, by people, as a leader was brought home to him, to a great extent, through dream therapy.

Going back to Lucille James — her type hostility appears in a large number of people and it takes time to help a person deal with his hostility and feel his way through it. It takes a lot of time to live but what a time of living a person can have who will work through the hostility and find a way out to being a true person with a meaningful life. What a world of difference this makes and what a difference in the world this makes to every person who enters into the venture of being real.

Dreams often deal with feelings of hostility and the recalling of the dream helps the counselor and counselee to understand the causes.

THE USE OF DREAMS IN COUNSELING AS SUGGESTED BY RICHARD MCKAY

FOLLOW THESE STEPS:

1. Have the counsellee tell the dream in narrative fashion.
2. Have the counsellee go back over the dream in detail so that counsellee and counsellor are aware of each detail. Ex.: Where was counsellee? What was counsellee doing? What was happening to the counsellee? Note such details as facts which date the dream. Ex.: "We were living in the big house where we lived when my mother died." The house dates the dream.
3. The dream is a transparancy. Now ask the counsellee to place it overlay fashion over her life story as she has already told it. Where does it fit?
4. Squeeze out the meaning of the dream — conceptualize the insights.
5. The counsellee may use the dream for further understanding.
6. The counsellor may use the dream to diagnose how well the counsellee is doing in insight development and assimilation — also her effectiveness in dealing with personal conflicts. Ex.: "Do you mean my mother's death is still influencing my attitude toward life?"
7. Gradually, the counsellee should learn to interpret dreams herself — leaning less and less upon the counsellor for help with the dream.
8. Caution: One dream in isolation from other dreams and the personality of the counsellee doesn't mean much. The counsellor should encourage the counsellee to write down dreams as soon as she awakes and to look for patterns in a number of dreams.
9. Caution: The dream is a tool ... not an end in itself.

Richard McKay

CHAPTER XV

"EVERYBODY IS AGAINST ME!"

The most import thought I ever had was that of my individual responsibility to God.
— *Daniel Webster*

Hope is like the sun, which, as we journey toward it, casts the shadow of our burden behind it.
— *S. Smiles*

Because of some disputes and arguments taking place in one of the departments, it was suggested it might be a good idea for the Chaplain to see Mike Jameson. Mike was six feet, two inches, very robust young man, but wherever he was assigned responsibility some kind of confusion would begin to get started around him. He was constantly in conflict with others. He was asked to come by for a little chat. His first response was quite vindictive and rebellious.

"Was it that you thought I might be part of the problem? Can't you see if everybody would let me alone and tend to their own business, we wouldn't be having any conflicts? Everybody is against me. It's been that way all my life. I just can't understand why everybody is against me. I'm the one that's always wrong. I'm the one that's always blamed for everything regardless of what takes place."

"Mike, let's just talk about things and see possibly where there might be some blame on both sides. You see, in almost any situation every person can find some places where he might be able to help out the situation and maybe find some small blame that's on himself."

"You mean you're not blaming me 100% wrong?"

"No, I don't believe anybody is 100% wrong."

"Well, you're the first one I ever saw that didn't blame me as being the one who was 100% wrong.

"The thing of it is really that everybody is against me. I just can't understand why, but everybody's against me. We had it tough all of our lives and now I am responsible for taking care of my mother. She doesn't have anybody to take care of her. She doesn't have anybody to be responsible for her. I find it difficult to make things go."

"Have you ever taken time to think through what it might be that makes you so demanding and impulsive toward other people? You know, psychiatrists have been able to study through different patterns of human behaviour and find out that when somebody has a tendency to fly off with temper outbursts, like to drive fast, and do impulsive things on the spur of the moment and if they do not like to stay with a job because they feel it is not worthwhile and feel unloved and if people don't give in to you, there is a strong possibility that you're reacting to over-submissiveness of your parents. Next to being rejected by your parents, this is the most common pattern of behaviour among parents that brings some unhealthy emotions among their children. Would you mind being honest in answering these questions? Did your parents kind of let you have your way as you came along? Did you really have an opportunity to decide what you wanted to do and when you wanted to do it?"

"Yes, that's true, but what does that have to do with me now? Just because I want to change jobs and never have stayed at a place very long, why will that have anything to do with my being regarded as a trouble maker? Why would my drinking, over-eating, driving too fast, and wasting money have anything to do with the way they treated me?"

"I'm just telling you that this is something that has been found out in testing people that it might be something because of what we've found out that you might be interested in. You know, everybody lives in a world of reality or unreality and *the more reality that can come into a person's world the more that he can learn how to deal with himself.* One of the outstanding psychiatrists that has used this approach in helping people to see themselves and to do a better job in life is a Dr. Hugh Missildine. Let me just give two or three things that he says that might be of help to you. You see, this is what somebody else is saying and not what I'm saying, so don't feel that it's something that I'm doing to pick on you. Dr. Missildine says impulse has driven people frequently to infringe on the feelings and rights of others because these people are accustomed to following their impulses — unreservedly they often start to find that others have been hurt by their temper outbursts or lack of consideration because they live in a moment — they actually tend to be blindly unaware of the feelings of others. When it comes to matters of love, this type of person tends to be a dictator and his partner is only a slave. The ideas or suggestions of others are not recognized and understood and considered desirable. Their over-eating, drinking, floundering, temper tantrums, wreckless business ventures, and spending infringe on the rights of others. Often, they are frantically exploded toward others. These people also are unable to keep a job and move toward adult goals even though they sincerely say they want to achieve them. They are easily distracted and diverted from these goals. The impulsiveness endlessly side tracts them because it prevents recognition of the distraction as something which can prevent achievement of the adult goal. Now since they are easily diverted from finding satisfaction in the persistent application of their efforts, in the slow often difficult progress toward adult goals, certain individuals are endlessly hunting immediate impulse satisfaction.

"Do you think any of this describes you?"

"Yes, it describes me to a tee, but I don't know what to say. In fact, it just kind of surprises me. I hadn't thought that because of as a child that my parent's attitude toward me as one of over-submissiveness that this would have a kind of an effect on me. You're the first person that's ever made sense. I always have been thought of as being an intelligent, witty person, having gentle poise, and always have been able to make friends but this other thing is something that has been a great bother to me. Any new job soon loses its appeal. I do find myself not interested in my job and find myself using caustic language with the people I work with. This stuff about eating and drinking is true of me too. But, I have always blamed other people instead of myself. I've even felt that God was against me. My mother is a very religious person and it just seems that everybody has been against me and I really hadn't stopped to think about being any of my own particular problem or that I had anything to do with it. I've always felt that I was imposed upon. I've often asked why is it that everybody's against me. Why is it that I have to do everything – it just seems to always fall back on me. What do you think I can do about it?"

"One of the ways that you can do something about it is to begin accepting responsibility for yourself. After all, whatever your parents have done or failed to do in your life you are a man now. You have to become a parent to yourself. You have to talk to yourself somewhat as you would talk with anybody else in this situation. You've seen from what we've discussed. Here's a man, who has spent his life in studying human behaviour patterns. He's been able to detect these things. This is the kind of analysis that he would give to someone who is acting as you do. This is a scientific evidence and it looks as though it might be something that would be practical to apply to your life."

"That makes sense. You know I felt that all you were trying to do was just get me to kind of be a good boy so to speak, and I've heard enough of that kind of stuff. Some of my relatives have said 'why don't you be good. Why don't you do this. You're supposed to do this and I just go out and do a little worse when they tell me that.' But, I've caught something from our conversation which makes sense and that is that it's my life and I'm betting on this thing and after all, I'm the one that has to live with myself and do something about myself. For some reason or the other what you said today makes sense and I'm going to think it over. I really believe that you're concerned about me and want to help me. I never have believed that before. I've rebelled against life because I thought everybody was against me. I didn't realize that it was an emotional thing."

"This is something everybody has to realize. Every person thinks that he already understands himself and that he's all one person — but you see you aren't all one person. You're many persons and you find yourself going in so many directions that there comes a time when you do have to begin to be conscious of these unconscious influences. Your life is guided mostly by emotions and this is something that everyone has to face up to and recognize. Not many people have any idea of the fact that they are living by their emotions and that their emotions are having an effect on them, but people live by emotions and not by ideas. The generality of mankind uses ideas only to justify or explain a way to decisions based largely on emotions. You take children for example, they are really fond of riddles because it's the only form of interjection to which they know the answers and their parents do not. A riddle is the child's way of getting back at the condescension of adults. We're just kind of going in circles right now and let's go about this by going back into your life and letting you talk out the things which really concern you and as we talk through these things you'll begin to find yourself."

As Mike talked about his home background, his economic background, his educational background, his social background, many clues began to come out as to why he was acting as he did and he began to see himself. *First,* he saw that he was *responsible* for his life being what it was and that he must accept responsibility for it. *Second,* he realized that there were certain guides that he could accept for his life which enable him to get insight and to why he acted as he did and that he was acting as he later called himself a baseball brat a term which he had always rebelled at before. *Third,* as he began to discover things about himself; he began to make forward steps toward other people in being friendly to them and seeking to understand them. *Fourth,* he began to see that it wasn't people against him, but the fact that he was mad at himself all the time and that was keeping him upset because he didn't like himself he thought people didn't like him. *Fifth,* he began to get real joy out of working with himself even though progress was slow and he often got discouraged but he began to get a real joy out of living. *Sixth,* he began to find for himself a religious base for his life and through this overcome some of his basic impulsiveness. Through prayer, he began to find a means of control in his life and be more concerned about others.

Most people revolt against their own humanity and in so doing have a tendency to blame everyone else for their discomfort.

There are some facts of emotional and mental maturity:

1. Life is a struggle for everyone. There is no plateau where anyone can withdraw from adjustment within himself and also with the rest of the world.

This struggle exists as one chooses whom he will hate and whom he will love; whether he will do what he wants to do or what he should do; whether to be selfish or unselfish; whether to be moral or immoral; whether to be childish or adult.

As he is fighting these inner struggles, he must also find his way in his world.

2. One must find security in his environment by balancing emotional stresses with emotional supports.

In meeting the two basic needs for his security, on inner harmony and peace, and to love and be loved, each person sets goals for what he will attain and do. There are so many facets of the human personality one can carry over and support a minor insecurity of the other. If one does not develop completely, it doesn't ruin the investor. Insecurity in a job can be overcome by sufficient support in the home in encouragement, love, reassurance, and confidence until the job becomes better.

3. Satisfaction, fun, and meaning in life are necessary to good emotional and mental health.

Too many are going through an apathetic, boresome existence thinking 'they will enjoy life later. This never happens — that time just never arrives. Husband and wives plan to make up for lack of proper attention and care.

The best thing to do is begin to live now by discovering a meaningful life. Learn to relax, play, and work. One without the others will not bring satisfaction.

THOUGHTS FOR CONSIDERATION

1. Everyone has some wrong emotional behavior and reactions that carries over from childhood.
2. Each person must accept the responsibility for his own actions and become a good parent to himself.
3. It is impossible to describe a normal person for there is no one pattern for one to follow.
4. All people have eccentricities and neurotic symptoms.
5. The two energy drives that make individuals go are aggressiveness and the desire to be loved.
6. It is the aggressive drive that causes difficulties. Because of the hostile and destructive element it causes most problems.
7. Mature love never hurts anyone. Smothering love, binding love, jealous love, and insecure love are harmful and become problems.

CHAPTER XVI

"BETTER MEN OR BITTER MEN"

Will is character in action.
— *William McDougall*

Remember that your will is likely to be crossed every day, and be prepared for it by asking only for God's will.
— *Fuller*

We are but the instruments of heaven; our work is not design, but destiny.
— *Owen Meredith*

Ross had come to a place in his life when he felt that God was speaking to him to commit his life to Him and to do something in a definite way that God wanted him to do in fulfilling God's purpose for his life. He decided that he would talk it over with the Chaplain. The Chaplain told him that he may not feel that his choice today was important, but that when he was forty-five he would be a very bitter man and a hard man or he would be a better man by the start that he made now and by the way that he began to let God have His plan in his life. He then told him the story of how a man in one of the large cities of the United States had drawn a plan for eliminating all of the slums of that particular city. If the city had followed that plan for the next ten years, then it would have eliminated all of the slums, but the leaders of the city decided not to follow it – twelve years later that city was the very center of destruction and violence and the slum areas had become intolerable. The Chaplain went on to explain that this is the parable of life and a person can determine by the choices he makes whether he is going to let God come into his life in such a way and guide his life to make him the person that he wants to be ten years from now or he will become a slum within himself – one that will be intolerable – one that will be of violence and he will be a bitter person, but he has a choice to be a better person.

So it is in having a faith of believing that you can now begin to be a person that you desire which enables one to begin this road that brings understanding, love, insight, and the kind of a life that a person wants to have. Ross had always wanted to follow a certain pattern of life. He wanted to be what his daddy had been. Because his father had died, he wanted to carry out his father's business and make a success of it.

This often happens in grief in that a member of the family, sometimes the wife or a son or a daughter, feels the need of identifying so much with that parent or with that husband that the life is given to living out the life of a deceased rather than the life of the living. Ross was determined that he was going to be the president of the corporation just like his father had, but this will not work – trying to live another person's life. Ross had to learn how to live his life.

"I do not see why it is so important to be what God wants you to be. After all, every person has a free choice of deciding what he will be in life and since he does have that free will, it seems that I could go ahead and make this choice without being a bitter man."

"Some part of what you said is true. There is a will within man that must be dedicated to God's will before that life can ever fulfill God's purpose. Before any one is born into this world, each person has a specific place that he is to fill. If he doesn't fill that place, then he is getting in the way – he is a part of the problem rather than a part of the solution. Just imagine a coach trying to have a football team that everytime when the tackle was supposed to carry out his assignment he would get back in the backfield and try to carry the ball. Now how long would he last on a team?"

"He wouldn't last very long – any coach would pull him out. Are you saying if I don't play life God's way that God's going to pull me out of life – that he is going to kill me – that he's going to let me die or he's going to punish me in some way?"

"No, I'm not saying that God is going to punish you. You'll be punishing yourself. If the tackle doesn't carry out his assignments, he is the one that's making the team lose and he's the one that is making the point of ridicule. It isn't somebody else that's making him do it. I'm not saying that God is going to pull you out of life – that he is going to kill you; however, there are some people who lose their lives because they are not being obedient to God's will and they are at a place where they shouldn't be – they're not listening to God and something tragic can happen to their lives. God does seek to guide our lives in such a way that these things do not take place. Of course, there are many people who are in God's will when somebody else is not in God's will and when that other person calls for them to be killed. But, this isn't the point. The point is whether you want to have inner peace within yourself – whether you want to develop the inner resources within yourself and if this is what you want in life, then the only person who can bring these to your life is God and you must determine as a young man whether or not you want to fulfill the purpose that you were placed here on this earth, or whether you want to just continually go against that which is best for yourself. After all, there is just one person who can see all of life and how it fits. There is only one person who is the master architect for all the world and that is God. You say you believe in God. You say that you know that He has come into your heart and life, but next thing to decide is whether or not you want Him to be Lord of your life which means He's your boss. That He's the one that gives directions to your life. That He is the one that makes it possible for you to have this inner peace and strength that is so meaningful. This is what I'm talking about."

"You mean that God is not going to make me do that which I

don't want to do."

"No, it's only when you cooperate with God and decide within yourself. You see everything with God begins by your being willing for God to take your life and make it what He wants it to be. You see, sin in its real significance and its basic meaning is your having your way with your life rather than letting God have His way with your life."

"I hadn't thought about it that way. Is that what it is? Then it is no wonder that a man has such a struggle is it? I always thought of sin not doing this — not doing that — sin was going out and getting drunk or committing some immoral acts sexually or stealing and that type of thing. I hadn't thought about sin being that which means having my way with my life rather than letting God have His way. Are you saying the Ten Commandments then are a guide to help us to find meaning to life rather than being something that says to us — 'this you got to do'."

"Yes, that's right, they are a guide for our lives to bring us into meaning and happiness the same as anything in life. We have certain guides to lead us to know how to play the game or how to carry on certain work and how to relate to people. And the Sermon on the Mount then carries the Ten Commandments to their highest meaning and shows within them how you can have the power within your life; the strength within your life for these to take place."

"That does put everything in a different prospective. I don't know why I hadn't seen that before. If God has a purpose for my life then that means that I am meaningful to Him and that I am significant to Him. I don't know why, but I just never had thought of my life being very important to God. I never had thought about the fact that God had a purpose for my life like He does everybody else for big men and for the great people who have accomplished so much."

"Yes, Ross, I think that is one of the greatest joys in religion is knowing that in God's sight that everybody is somebody and that God has just as definite plan for your life as He did for Moses — as He did for any of the great prophets in the Old Testament — as He did for those that He later called to be Apostles and work with Jesus and as He did for the Apostle Paul. You see, everybody has his place and when you fill your place, then there is not any competition between people. For you see, when people are in God's will there's no competition. You're not in competition with anybody else. You're in competition with yourself as to the person that you can be. There isn't anyone else that can be in competition with you if you're in God's will. And, the point is not whether you are measuring up as some other person measures up to but whether you're measuring up as to what you can be and to your potential."

"That does make sense, but it's just a new thought to me. I'll have to think it over. I'll have to think it over. It's so confounded profound, it kind of jars me."

"It jars anybody when you come to think of the fact that the God who created the world — the God who is over everybody has specific interest in everyone and that everybody is somebody and that He has a specific place for each one to fill in life. This jars anybody. For all of a sudden instead of your being just a little speck out here, all of a sudden you realize that God needs you even as much as you need God and that God has no other way of doing what He wants to do here except what we are willing to let Him do through us. For you see, it's not in going out and trying to do God's work, but it's letting God work through us that everything takes on a new meaning for us and for those that we meet each day. That's why all of this is so important. So you see, everybody has a choice of being a bitter man or adapting for himself a plan that will end up eventually in bitterness or end up in wishing he would have been and that he could be at that time what it would have been possible if he had made the right choice at the right time in life. So nothing is so important as making the right choices."

It took Ross a period of two years to decide within himself what he was going to do and how. He began to study intensely in certain books. He began to talk with people and get into discussion groups where there were people who were searching as he was in trying to find within himself that what he wanted to do. But, he did after a period of two years make a commitment of his life to God's will.

"I came to have the deepest peace in my life when I decided to give my will to God and let Him control it. I realize that God has a purpose for every life — not just for preachers or missionaries, but for everybody and that every person can have such a close relationship to God that God does give divine guidance to that life. I found out that when I resolved to let God have control of my life whether I fell a million times or not and realized that was one reason that I didn't want to get started on it. I had fear of failure, but when I resolved that I was going to let Him have His way, regardless of how I failed or whether I failed, that I was going to get started on that journey — that did something to me. The second thing that I did was to have discipline for my life. I found out that I had to have a discipline for my life that was different because everyone has his own particular discipline that he follows. I began to spend an hour a day in talking with God — reading the Bible and in contemplation and in reflection; I found contemplated prayer to be very meaningful. The third thing was that I did begin to do what you suggested in having a faith to believe that I could be what I really wanted to be. You know, I saw that this was what I really desired in my heart — that I was fearful of entering into something saying publicly that I am going to commit my life to God's control and let Him make me what He wants me and by His help, I will fulfill his purpose. I felt when I did that publicly that somehow it put me on the spot, but thank God, even though I am on the spot, that there is a God who is big enough and strong enough to help me through it."

THOUGHTS FOR CONSIDERATION

1. Don't underestimate the value of religion in the daily life.
2. Reading the Bible, prayer, and participating in religious worship and discussions bring springs of joy within the heart.
3. Any person is deprived and destitute when he does not have what religion offers.
4. Take every opportunity to get solace from a church and a minister.
5. God has a purpose for every life.
6. Everybody is somebody in God's sight.
7. Meaning to life comes only in God's will for that person.

CHAPTER XVII

"I'M SURE GLAD I DID"

Gratitude is not only the memory but the homage of the heart — rendered to God for His goodness.
— *N. P. Willis*

He who remembers the benefits of his parents is too much occupied with his recollections to remember their faults.
— *Beranger*

"Chaplain, I'll never know how to thank you enough for urging me to be reconciled with my mother and to go and express to her the deep love that I actually felt for her. It's a silly thing, but it often happens in families when you get away from them or in anger say things that cause the family circles to be broken. It was really my rebellion in wanting to have my own way that caused me to leave home in the first place. I know my mother had the best intentions, but she was blind at times and wanted me to be in at such early hours that I couldn't be with the other young people and take part in the things they did, so I just left home and made my own way now for ten years. I went on to college and worked my way through. Even though I went back to the home town, I wouldn't even speak to my mother. I made no pretense of seeking to have any kind of reconciliation. If it hadn't been for listening to some of the chapel services and the emphasis that you have given on forgiveness, love and understanding, I never would have done the thing which really in my heart I know I wanted to do. I was just plain too stubborn to acknowledge my part in our misunderstanding. I realize now it would have been better if I had gone on and had done what she requested regardless of whether I was able to keep up with all the rest of the young people of our day. Actually, what they did after the hours that my mother wanted me in probably were not too conducive to my own welfare anyway.

"It was just the accepted thing among our gang that most of our partying was from eleven until about two o'clock in the morning and my mother just insisted that I be in at eleven o'clock – under no circumstance later than twelve. This just cut me out and made the girls think that I was a square and became kind of a joke that little Larry Mitchell was a mama's boy and had to come home when she said.

"I realize my father's death when I was fifteen caused greater anxiety by my mother concerning what I did. I was the only boy in the family and the oldest child and the three sisters that were younger than I did not help bring any emotional support to my mother. But, I was just too proud and was thinking of myself when I decided that I'd take off.

"I guess one of the big things that I was trying to show off on was that I could take care of myself and I did send money home to my mother to help with the children and continued to do that and she has always written letters of gratitude for what I'd done. I have been very fortunate in making money during the summers. I would go out and work as a salesman for a book company and was often able to make six, seven or eight thousand dollars which would make it possible for me to go on through school. I have made as high as ten thousand dollars and then I would always work during the school year so even when I was in college I was making as much money as some young executives make. I always shared that and the family did have enough to live on. In this, I too took great pride that I was doing something for somebody that didn't have the good judgement of knowing how to handle me and how to deal with me.

"But the thing that I became to realize in your messages, especially that series of messages you had on love, was that a mother's love is one of the most beautiful things that a young man can experience and that my attitude was completely wrong. I resolved that I was going to run my life my way. I was going to get what I wanted out of this life. I was going to get what I wanted as early as I could and I wasn't going to let anybody stop me. I suppose the insecurity that I felt when my father died, and we had little to live on, had something to do with my resolve to make success. See, my daddy was a good man, but he was a poor manager and we never did have the things that we really wanted so I resolved that I was going to make a success out of my life. I was going to make money and I suppose that's part of what built such a strong spirit with me, but I was determined to make a success."

"This desire to succeed and to be successful is in many ways the strongest desire that's in a man. A woman has the desire to be secure and probably a part of your mother's reason for what she was saying to you and requiring of you was for her own security. In a sense, when you were out at certain times she didn't know what was going to happen to you and if something had happened to you it would have broken her heart especially so close to your father's death. This drive in you to be a success is considered to be the strongest drive in man from the standpoint of his natural disposition, instincts and patterns of behaviour."

"Yes, I realize that this is a strong drive in me that I didn't understand at first, but now that I am one of the top junior executives and making what I am, I realize that this is not nearly so important as being in the right relationship with your family. I also recognize that my mother's insecurity was a deep factor in the way that she felt. But, in this chapel message that you mentioned before Mother's Day, you were talking on the debt that we owe to our parents and how important and how meaningful it is not just to the mother, but to the son or daughter who is able to express genuine gratitude. I had never really thought of how important it was to the person to have a sense of gratitude – to have a real sense of appreciation for what had been done for them. After all, she is the one that brought me into the world and when nobody else cared for me, she took care of me. She made it possible for me to have a sense of love as a child because my parents did give me love. It's just one of those things that's like the pitcher in the ball game – I got to listening to the crowd and almost threw away the game that counted so much. But, any way I got to reflecting on this of how that the sin of ingratitude is probably one of the greatest sins that anybody could commit and I realize that is where you had me because of all my unwillingness to be reconciled and to ever admit that I was wrong. It wasn't my place to be confessing my mother's sins and where she failed, but it was my place to be confessing my own sins where I had failed and if I was really going to be the man that I could be that it would begin with my taking the initiative of being truly reconciled to my mother. My mother told me many times how she would like for us to be close again as we were when I was a little boy and as the young teenager. She has made every effort for us to be close and be reconciled.

"Anyway, the thing that I'm trying to tell you is that I went home for Mother's Day and I told the girls that I wanted to talk with mother alone. We went into the little sewing room where she had spent so many hours making things for me and the other children where she worked her fingers to the bone in order that we might have clothes to wear and look as nice as other kids who had so much more. And, just sitting in that room got to me emotionally – I broke down and I said, 'Mother, I've been a fool – I'm not trying to say that you were right or that you were wrong about wanting me to be in at a certain hour and our having this big fuss that caused me to leave. I just want you to know that I know that I was wrong and Mother I'm so sorry. I want you to forgive me.' And I went as I used to do as a little boy, got on my knees at her lap and I cried and I'm not ashamed that I cried. I wept tears of repentance – tears of remorse of what I'd done to this dear mother who had given so much and who had sighed so much for me. I'd expected her to be perfect to be so understanding and my definition of perfection was that she recognized what I needed and what I wanted to do as though I was perfect in what I wanted to do. God only knows the joy that is in my heart by doing that which was right toward her. She put her hand over on my head just like she used to do when I was a little boy. All of a sudden I felt warm inside. I felt a glow. I felt a joy that I hadn't felt in ten years. Then I got up and held mother in my arms and we both wept. We talked for hours – then it was time to eat. Since she hadn't had time to fix a meal, I took everybody out for lunch that day and I told the girls how I felt. Two of them were married and I told their husbands. As we sat together as a family, then mother told us that she was going to have to go to the hospital the next week for an examination.

"None of us knew it at the time, but the doctor had already told her that she had cancer. Six months from that day – you know the rest of the story – for you know that my mother died. What a joy it was to me to be at that funeral service – knowing not only that my mother was in heaven but that the blessings and joys of heaven were in my heart because I was in the right relationship with God and the right relationship with my mother. Oh, I'm so glad that I did make things right. I'm sure glad I did."

THOUGHTS FOR CONSIDERATION

1. A great sense of gratitude builds character and a happy heart.

2. Putting action to carry out the impulses to express appreciation will bring joy to all involved.

3. Reestablishing family ties is always a wise decision.

4. When a wrong choice is made in human conduct, the emotions begin to react and will not accept wrong behavior.

5. All emotional problems have a moral basis where the right road was missed in some way.

6. Being right within and in a right relationship with those near and dear is the foundation for emotional health and a sound religion.

7. There is a way that seems right to man but the end thereof is the way of death.

CHAPTER XVIII

"GOD IS NOT DEAD AFTER ALL"

The demand of the human understanding for causation requires but the one old and only answer, God.

— *Dexter*

They that deny God, destroy man's mobility; for clearly man is of him to the beasts by his body, and if he is not kin to God by his spirit, he is a base and ignoble creature.

— *Bacon*

Many industries have doctors that come to hold clinics and assist the nurse that is often available for whatever number of shifts that a particular corporation has.

Dr. Jim Bruce was a young doctor, the youngest member on the staff of doctors who worked for this particular corporation, and one day after he had seen everyone, he came into the office and with a spirit of arrogance remarked, "Chaplain, what if I told you I didn't believe in God — what would you think?"

The chaplain answered, "I would think that you didn't get along very well with your father."

Dr. Bruce's face showed great alarm and great surprise and he turned a little white and then a little green — seemed he wasn't going to be able to breathe for a little while.

"How in the hell did you know that. How did you know that I didn't get along with my father. How did you know that we're not on speaking terms even today?"

"Many times when a person says that he doesn't believe in God it means that he hasn't gotten along very well with his father and his barrier to his belief in God is his father. For if a person has not had good relationships with his father — it's pretty hard for him to believe in God. For somehow or the other we associate God with our earthly father. If you do not have a good father image, then it's pretty rough to have a good image of God or any kind of belief in God."

"My dad is the most stubborn jackass in all the world. He can't get along with anybody and particularly he can't get along with me."

"Well, you know 50% of your own reactions and feelings in life come from your father and 50% from your mother so it could be that you and your daddy might be a little bit alike."

"Don't tell me that. I'm not like him in any respect."

"I'm not saying that you and your daddy are alike. I just said that you might be but any way 50% of the way you feel and react in life, 50% of the qualities you have come from your father and his side of the family, and 50% from your mother."

"I just dislike my father very much. I don't feel that he has been fair toward my mother or toward any of us. He always wanted us to jump at the snap of his finger and he never had any time for us when we were growing up and yet he has expected us to think he is great and give loyalty to him when I don't feel he deserves it.

"Anytime that anything about him and his relationship with the family comes up, he is always bragging about how much money he spent on putting me through school — that he gave me the best education that any person could have — he sent me through college — he sent me through medical school — he sent me through eight years of residency and special training and he wants full credit for everything that I am. I'm not going to give him credit for anything. He thinks because he gave us money that he gave us love."

"Money is an indication of love and some people do feel that when they give money that the other person should realize that they love them, but that isn't enough. Naturally, a boy or girl wants love from their parents and wants it expressed in words and in other ways that have a special meaning."

"That's right. That's what I wanted from my daddy. I wanted him to take time to go hunting with me. I wanted him to take time to go with me to the fairs and to go with me to the occasions where other boys' fathers always took them. My dad would get some man who had a son that I ran around with or liked, but also did not have the money, to take us and he would pay for all the expenses. Of course, the man was glad to take us because it made it possible for him to go to a lot of places he wouldn't have been able to go otherwise. How do you think I felt sitting there with somebody else's daddy and my daddy never went with me. He never went with me a time to a football game when I was a boy. Now, when it became the time that I began to play football, he would come out and watch me play and then brag about what I'd done and it was just a chip off the old block and all that stuff. My dad was seldom at home. He was always gone, and it was very difficult for us to have a vacation together. He'd plan and tell us that he was going to take us on a vacation and then at the last minute some business would come up that he had to take care of so he would go ahead and send the children and mother on somewhere and maybe he would fly down for the weekend or fly down and come back with us or something like that while the rest of the families were on the beach or in the mountains having a good time together. When the rest of the kids had their daddy along with them — mine wasn't there. I just never have felt like I had a daddy. When you start talking about God being like your father, well when you've had an absentee father you've got an absentee God too. How can you believe in something that you never do see and never is around."

"Doctor, you have given a pretty good description of what

173

ordinarily you would have studied in some medical schools. What medical school did you attend?"

When he mentioned the school he attended, it was not one of those that did have courses in behavioral sciences and courses in the human relations training such as is given at Bowman Gray Medical School in Winston-Salem, North Carolina. There, not only do they have a staff of qualified doctors dealing with the medical students in these areas, but also have an ordained minister in the field of behavioral sciences. More and more the medical schools are seeing the importance of training the doctors with the adequate knowledge of sex and human behaviour that they might be able to carry this over in their medical practice and be able to recognize these needs in people. More and more, the schools are giving medical training rather than just the scientific approach and are giving the human approach too.

This discussion began a close relationship with Dr. Bruce and he in turn began to have this understanding of himself which made it possible for him to begin to initiate an understanding of his father and beginning to bring about a relationship with him and his father. More than this was the fact that he began to get interested in a serious study of doctors getting together and engaging in religious discussions. He formed a group amond the doctors that has been very beneficial and has opened the way for these doctors to take vital leadership in their own churches.

One day, Dr. Jim Bruce came in and said, "Well, Chaplain, God isn't dead after all — He is very much alive and I am so thankful that I've come to experience this personally and have it now as a vital part of my life and family. It's great isn't it — God isn't dead after all."

THOUGHTS FOR CONSIDERATION

1. Many problems concerning belief are emotional rather than intellectual.

2. Usually when a person describes the kind of God he does not believe in, he is telling about a God that very few could accept.

3. Much of the disfavor toward institutionalized religion is due to the poor influence and the failure to put religion into practice.

4. All youth are idealistic regardless of what their childhood might have been.

5. Everyone would benefit from small discussion and renewal groups who deal with reality and have great compassion.

6. God does not need defending, but man's behavior needs to be changed through God's grace.

7. Come and let us reason together says the Lord.

CHAPTER XIX

"SHE'S SO TOUGH"

Bachelors' wives and old maids' children are always perfect.
— *Chamfort*

Perfection does not exist; to understand it is the triumph of human intelligence; to expect to possess it is the most dangerous kind of madness.
— *Alfred de Musset*

Sue Jones came in one day so upset it was very hard to distinguish what she was trying to talk about. "I don't know what I'm going to do about Pat Simmons. She's so tough and hard to work with about every detail in the office. There's nothing that I can do to please her. There's no way that anybody can work with her. It's just simply impossible. Something has got to be done. The other girls asked me to come and talk with you and see what you could do about it. After all, you're the chaplain and you're supposed to have the answers for everything."

"Now, Sue, that's a pretty big job saying the chaplain has the answer for everything. I do believe that whatever situations are faced that something can be done about it. If those concerned are willing to listen and to seek for what is best, there's a reason why everybody acts as she does, so sometimes, the working conditions in an office are helped when we find out what it is that is bugging the person that seems upset. Is Pat upset all the time? She always seems very nice in talking with me and in being with the president and the other officers of the company."

"Yes, she can be just as nice as she pleases when she's around the president and other people. She seems to fit in well with them and carries out everything that they tell her to do. They think she's great, but she sure is tough to work with. When it comes to the rest of us, she can get along with the big brass and doesn't show out with them as she does with us. She always says that she has more work to do than she can get done and she tries to push us to do the same kind of work that she does. After all, Pat doesn't have a family like many of us, and she can stay and work over where we can't. It's just really tough. I mean it's tough and something has got to be done."

After thinking through the matter and because of having a good working relationship with Pat Simmons, I decided that the best thing to do was just to have a talk with her.

"Pat, how's everything going with you these days?"

"Pretty rough, Chaplain. Pretty rough. You know, we're right in the midst of our busiest time and I'm having a rough time getting these girls to function and get the work done. It seems they've always got problems or something bothering them all the time. It's hard to keep them up to their highest efficiency. I tell you, it's hard to find anybody these days that wants to work and really produce."

"Pat, how long have you been here with the company?"

"I've been here 15 years and I really do like it. I wish though that we could get better girls that I could depend on more to carry the things in the office."

"Pat, do you think your attitude toward the girls might have something to do with the amount that they are able to produce? You know, sometimes the very fact that the person who demands a lot out of them is as efficient as you are makes them feel inferior and makes it more difficult for them to work."

"I know that could be true, but they just don't put it out. I've always been taught to work. When I was a child I was taught to work. I've been taught to have everything in place and to make everything just right. My mother was a perfectionist in everything that she did and I guess I'm one too. Oh, I remember as a little child how careful she was about even our toilet training. She was just emaculate in everything concerning our toilet training. And was so careful to see that we went to the bathroom at the right time and just kept us on a particular schedule. She would often put us in the bathroom and make us stay until we did have some action. We went to the bathroom on schedule kinda like we did everything else on schedule. All along, we were taught to keep everything in place. I was never permitted to leave anything out at any time so I've just been reared to keep everything in place all the time. This is just my way of life. I just can't stand for things not to be in place and to be like they ought to be. I can't stand for people to do shoddy work. So often these girls are doing it."

"And what do you think about the best means of getting people to work? You know, many people do not have the same standards that you have and they have not had the benefit of knowing how to do work as you do. You think there might be a way of approaching them that might keep them from being so upset and at the same time instill confidence in them?"

"Well, I hadn't thought too much about that. I've just had my own way of doing things and I've tried to instill it into them and get them to do it."

"You see, this doesn't take into account that every person is a little bit different. Every person has to find his or her own way of functioning. I know that you've got to have certain routines to do your work. Are there times when you get overly tense in your work and get upset? I know that at times you seem to have headaches and other problems that are physical."

"Yes, I do get real tense and tied up and it takes a long time to get unwound. I push myself all the time to be on schedule and I time myself as to what I do to be that I do everything right and on time."

Pat is a good example of a person who has had strict toilet training and been brought up in a very strict way. Such a person has to be on time for everything. There's a compulsion to do things just exactly right. Everything about the house has to be kept in perfect order and the same about the office. This type of personality is very difficult to work with because the same demands that she makes on herself she makes on the other members of her family and those that she works with every day. In Pat's case, she did not have anyone else at home with her so she kept her house in meticulous order all the time and it disturbed her that she couldn't keep the office that way. She always stayed and got everything arranged just right on her desk and saw that everything was done for that day. Such a high expectancy of a person will begin to cause some physical disorders. There is a routine that can be established that a person can go by, but at the same time, there has to be a time to unwind. Because Pat has not done this, she was already developing a very impatient attitude toward others. This first session with her opened the door for other conferences and she began to see what was causing her to drive herself so much and act in such compulsion. She was much easier to get along with and was much easier to get things done with. The atmosphere of the office changed as the girls began to understand what she wanted done, how she wanted it done, and the fact that she was sympathetic with them. When she could have a true empathy by joining the human race and permit other people to be human as well as admitting to herself that she was a human being, or human becoming, everything changed for her. Her attitude and her associates.

Instead of being one as one who was so tough to get along with, she's now known as one whose personality and understanding is welcomed by everyone that comes in to her particular department. She also has had a better reception with the executives of the company because they were concerned with her perfectionist attitude about everything. She had gotten to where she would pick at them over things that they didn't do like she thought it ought to be done. This was exceeding her authority and beginning to get them upset with her.

Her perfectionism had poured over into all relationships with people and she wanted to take everyone over and remake them, reshape them, revamp them according to what she thought they ought to be. She realized that in a sense this was playing god and was a very unwholesome attitude in all of her relationships with other people.

One of the aspects that seemed to be a special help to Pat was realizing her need to confess her own problems, her own sins and distresses. Since she had been taught so long what she ought to be she tried to go ahead and act as though this was the kind of person she was.

"I'd always been told I was to be a certain kind of person; I was supposed to do this, I was supposed to do that, and that I was supposed to do it in a certain way. So, I got to where I would cover over my deficiencies and go ahead and act as though I was this kind of a person. I was hoping that any inadequacies in whatever my failures and shortcomings were I preferred to keep them out of sight so other people might think well of me. I felt that this standard that I had for myself was what I had to live up to in order to be accepted. I just couldn't think of people accepting me with my shortcomings; I found that this made it impossible for me to accept others. I couldn't accept my own faults and I couldn't accept faults in others. In talking with you and being in the other groups, where others have opened up and told about themselves, I see this is a common fault with all of us in our willingness to admit that we are part of the human race.

"I realize now that there is something in my own conscience which has been severly punishing me for letting my pride keep me from admitting I'm a part of the human race. When I began to cease to defend and assert myself and began to confess myself as fallible and a part of the human race, things really began to happen within myself. I found out that I was being kept subdued, and kept from being myself, that, really, instead of revealing myself, I was constantly concealing myself. I noticed in one of the messages that you gave to us, that you spoke of this as being one of the greatest tragedies of our days, that people were always trying to conceal themselves rather than to reveal themselves."

"Yes, Pat this is something that counselors have discovered that every person's secret has the effect of sin or guilt whether it's morally wrong or not. And it does provoke a concealment which isolates one from his other fellow beings in damaging ways by preventing her from living openly with others less her secret be exposed. When the inner feelings of life are shared it actually draws people together beneficially. But if it's a private secret, it has a destructive affect of aleinating a person from those around him. Even more destructive are the secrets hidden from yourself inducing these repressions that have set up a war of tension in the deeper recess of your personality.

"You also were concealing and withholding your emotions. Of course, there is a self-restraint in social discipline which is fine and which helps us in our achievement, but private self-restraint is as destructive as any secret. When you conceal something even from yourself, in deceptive ways that cover up and deny true feelings, living a lie separates you anxiously from others.

"Psychiatrists and psycoanalysts have discovered that this unwillingness to reveal yourself is as destructive as anything in life so this inner-cleansing that we call catharsis brings a cleansing of the secret emotions and brings you in to other people and this is the way that you are accepted and this is the way that you begin to live."

"I see now, and I can see how important it is. And I must admit that I am very grateful to these girls for coming to talk with you so that we could bring this thing to a head. You just don't know how relieved I am.

"I never realized how much fun it would be to be a human being. I really had never begun to live until I'd admitted that I was a part of the human race and got in with them. It's a great life. And I'm so grateful for it all. I just don't know how to thank you enough for what has taken place in my life. Every part of my being has come alive and the emotions that I pushed down for so long now have become a form of energy which makes every part of my work better. I just thank God, thank you and thank the rest for not giving up on me. I know that I must have been a real sour puss for everybody."

"Whatever you might have been, the main thing is what you are now. So enjoy it. God expects you to live it up all the time."

"That's what I'm doing. Letting God so direct my life, that I can live it the highest and best for each day. And I am just living it one day at a time. It's great to be alive, so great!"

THOUGHTS FOR CONSIDERATION

1. There isn't anyone qualified to hand out neat little prescriptions that can be guaranteed to cure all aches, pains, worries, and fears.

2. God does not give a spirit of fear but of power, love and a sound mind.

3. Smooth sailing in life does not depend on fancy formulas or panaceas, but on the craft (the human personality), the weather (the temper of associates), and the navigation (the skill in steering a wise course). — William C. Menninger.

4. Many times the emotions overrule the intelligence. All are sub-species of fear or love.

5. The four categories of behavior, instincts and emotions are sex, fear, anger, and wonder.

6. Anyone not stopping to examine where he is emotionally is making a serious mistake. He will bring his emotional immaturity into all his relationships with others.

7. Everyone can have a better life.

CHAPTER XX

"CHECKING YOURSELF OUT FOR ACTION"

Begin to be now what you will be hereafter.
— *St. Jerome*

The improvement of our way of life is more important than the spreading of it.
— *Charles A. Lindbergh*

Our great object in time is not to waste our passions and gifts on the things external that we must leave behind, but that we may cultivate within us all that we can carry into the eternal progress beyond.
— *Bulwer*

Every person is told by his doctor to take time to check up on his physical health. By people getting a physical check-up every six months or annually, they are often times able to discover something that would have developed into a very serious complication. This is true in the emotional, as well as the physical realm. There are many aspects of checking one's life to see what he has attained.

The question has been asked, "Who is normal?" This is difficult to answer. After all, doesn't everyone have something wrong with him? If people as a whole give the answer, they are often wrong. They called Jesus crazy.

When a doctor says, "You are well," it is true that the physical condition is not perfect, but those words sound wonderful.

There must be a definition of a normal person, even though many psychiatrists would say there is none.

A normal person is relatively free to choose, and because of this, is responsible for his decisions. There is no reason why a normal person should not be evaluated by the teaching of the Bible on right and wrong, sin, guilt, repentance, forgiveness, resentment, joy, happiness, sorrow, success and failure.

There are qualities in everyone which can be improved by the proper counseling and a greater participation in giving of self to the fellowship of the redeemed.

Who is a normal person? According to one psychiatrist, Dr. Edward Glover, of London, a normal person may be defined as being free of symptoms, unhampered by mental conflict, having a satisfactory work capacity, and being able to love someone other than himself.

The word "normal" is a relative term. What may be accepted behavior in one locality, may be considered abnormal or socially offensive in another community. However, there are certain definite characteristics that are common to the largest number of normal people. Persons who classify under the normal group should be able to meet the following requirements: [1]

1. They must be able to manifest evidence of emotional maturity, be able to establish a healthy detached relationship to their parents, be able to think and act as an adult, assume responsibility and be emotionally self-sustaining.

(The normal person is not a "leaner" but stands on his own two feet.)

2. The second requirement for earning the badge of normalcy is the ability to accept reality.

[1] Frank S. Caprio, M. D., *Living In Balance,* (New York, N. Y. Medical Research Press, 1951) pp. 14-20

3. The normal person is able to get along with almost everyone. (The secret of his adjustment to people lies in his ability to subject his emotions to the control of his intellect.)

4. The capacity to love someone or something is the fourth requisite for normal living.

5. The normal being has a philosophy of life that holds him up when the complications of daily living become too burdensome.

To sum this up, everyone with determination, by self-analysis or outside help, is capable of becoming normal if he makes a sincere effort to: first, achieve a state of emotional maturity (do not remain a family-slave); second, accept reality (work and earn a livelihood without complaint); third, allow the intellect to guide the emotions (getting along with others); fourth, cultivate the capacity for love (finding love within one's own heart and sharing it); fifth, adopt a system of thinking based on an appreciation of all that which is beautiful, for peace of mind, as well as a *joie de vivre* (joy of living).

There are ways that a person can check up as to how well adjusted he is. In a condensed form of his writing — "The Wisdom of Your Subconscious Mind" — which was published in the *Reader's Digest*, Dr. John K. Williams presented some definite suggestions that are of help in this particular area. The Greek philosopher Socrates taught his disciples: "Know Thyself." In this precept the ancients saw the process or law through which all success and happiness are attained.

If one is to "know" himself, he must keep in mind that life is a continuing struggle between two basic drives. Everyone knows the urge to live, the instinct of self-preservation which is back of almost everything he plans and does. He should remember that the opposite impulse, self-destruction, is also a part of his equipment. It seems absurd that one would enter into an even unconscious conspiracy to fail, but there is hardly any person who does not, in some fashion, deliberately cripple and thwart himself. Failures and disappointments belong to the life of every man and woman. Among the wise men of India there is a legend that when God was equipping man for his life journey, the attending angel was about to add the gift of contentment and complete satisfaction. But God would not permit such a thing to happen. He said, "If you give him that, you will rob him forever of the joy of self-discovery."

The mentally healthy man, according to Dr. Williams, accepts temporary defeats as inevitable experiences on the path to success. He does not believe that a person is a helpless puppet driven by subconscious instinctual desires and forces. The healthy person knows that he determines his own life, selects his own goal, and that no one, in the words of Tennyson, "walks with aimless feet."

Beyond this, there are certain characteristics suggested by Dr. Williams, that are, to a reasonable degree, found in any normal, mentally healthy person.

First, this person is able to deal with the demands of life. He is able to wait for the problems of each day and knows that the problems of tomorrow cannot be solved by worrying about them today. He tries to avoid problems before they arise, but there is a vast difference between planning and worrying. Problems are never solved by daydreaming or by running away, as the temptation always says to do. The healthy person challenges each new obstacle he meets, gives all he has to overcoming it, then is satisfied when he has done his best.

The second mark of the healthy person is that he likes himself. Good mental health and happiness are two sides of the same coin. This does not mean that a well-adjusted person is completely satisfied with himself. It simply means that deep down inside he has a healthy self-image. It is impossible for anyone to be constantly tearing down his life, and at the same time do creative and satisfactory work. If there is hate of self, there follows then the consequence of limiting the ability and also of destroying the physical and mental health.

A third suggestion, concerning the healthy person, is that he expects to like and trust other people, and he accepts the fact that others will like him. Such a person is tolerant of others' shortcomings just as he is of his own. He does not try to push people around, and he will not be pushed around himself. He has the capacity of loving other people, of thinking about their interests and well-being. His friendships are meaningful and lasting. As he has the capacity to accept other people, he is indicating that he has accepted himself as he is and is seeking to bring that self more and more into the authentic person which he is capable of being.

A fourth Characteristic of the healthy person is that he does not explode for little or no cause. When he gets mad, his anger is in proportion to what caused it. He experiences fear, hate, jealousy, guilt, worry, and frustrations as other people do, but he is not overcome by any of them. He has learned to resolve them in a way that they do not make him sick.

A fifth quality of this person is that he plans for the future. He has concepts of what he is to be and knows his future according to this. He does not know what will happen any more than anyone else does, but he does not fear that which he does not know. He knows that change is part of life, and he welcomes it. By seeking to plan for his future, he is able to have a part of his own destiny and to bring it into line with the purpose and will of God. Many people are not able to get anywhere because they do not know where they want to go. Every life must have its goals.

A sixth thing that the healthy person is able to do is that he makes his own decisions and then accepts responsibility for making them. When he makes a mistake, he acknowledges it. But instead of blaming someone else or crying over it, he resolves never to make that same error again. He is thereby able to profit from his mistakes.

In short, the mentally healthy person, according to Dr. Williams, does whatever he undertakes to the best of his ability. If the result is not perfect, he does not let anxiety rob him of his happiness but tries to do better the next time. He tries for the goals he thinks he can achieve through his own abilities and doesn't ask for the moon. He is able to enjoy life.

Another aspect of life where there needs to be a checkup is for a person to see if he has some honest convictions. There is a great need for people to have convictions. Convictions determine the course of life and enable one to become a person. It is a very healthy thing for a person to believe that he has a part in carving out his own future, and that somehow in spite of poverty, hostile environment, circumstances, and situations, he can have a good and wholesome life. If one accepts the attitude, that is so prevalent, of passive resignation, life will cease to have any true meaning.

The famous pioneer American psychologist, Dr. William James, urged everyone to make efficient plans for his future. "The idea is father to the deed," according to Dr. James. No one can expect to accomplish much through his action unless he has previously formulated a constructive plan. Far too many people have thrown in the sponge and act as if they were rudderless ships in the onward stream of civilization.

This is not the plan of God. God has given to every person a brain to be used as a rudder so that he can plan his work and then work out his plan.

By carrying out his 100 per cent convictions, an individual is able to put vitality and meaning into his life that has a ring of delight and a joy of expression.

R. C. Stevenson has written: "An aim in life is the only fortune worth the finding and it is not to be found in foreign lands — but in the heart itself."

A fourth check-up is how much courage does one have. Courage is the response that one makes at a time of fear, so that his fears do not become unwholesome, but are used as emotions to add strength to life. This courage is seen in the gallant and marvelous way in which ordinary people do their monotonous jobs, in parents who give themselves so unselfishly in the rearing of handicapped children, in those who live in never-ending pain without hating those who have good health, in adults who stalwartly give up malice and suspicion by teaching themselves to relax and trust. This is the kind of courage that is really necessary in the hearts of people.

June Callwood tells of a patient in a Canadian veterans' hospital who became a legend because of all the pain he endured.[1] A sniper's bullet in Korea had smashed his hip and sent a hundred splinters of bone through his body. When his dressings were changed, he bent steel rods in his hands and screamed. Yet he commented that he was better off than the amputees. The amputees, however, considered themselves much more fortunate than the blind, and the blind felt sorry for the paraplegics. The paraplegics didn't regard themselves as courageous — the really brave man, in their viewpoint, was the one dying quietly of kidney cancer. But that patient was convinced that he would recover!

Courage is a private thing, according to Miss Callwood, and everyday heroism seldom reaches visibility.

"Our banal daily life makes banal demands on our patience, our devotion, endurance, and self-sacrifice," wrote philosopher-psychoanalyst, Carl Jung, "which we must fulfill modestly and without heroic gestures, and which actually need a heroism not seen from without."

All growth in the human personality requires this kind of invisible courage. When one is able to give up a longheld prejudice, resentment, or hatred, it is like an amputation. Yet, to go on, human beings must valiantly keep shedding themselves of that which is negative, harmful, and frustrating. While some people are able to move agilely, to absorb new information and points of view, and to let go of the structures and patterns of life which have been very meaningful to them, there are others for whom such advancement is very scary.

Admiral "Bull" Halsey made a famous comment on heroes.

---

[1] *Reader's Digest,* March 1965, pp. 117

"There are no great men," he said, "only great challenges that ordinary men are forced by circumstances to meet."

Few great challenges crackle with the unmistakable drum-roll of destiny, states June Callwood, yet, inconspicuously, courage makes its daily triumph over misery, death, frustration and injustice.

She goes on to state that courage in its highest form, moral courage, is what makes a man indestructible. And there is a momentum to it. Each act of courage adds to man's faith in himself, in the purpose and dignity of all life. By each brave act he enlarges his ability to be brave — and eventually the process is irreversible.

Courage enables one to go ahead in what he believes to be right, regardless of its acceptance by other people. This does not mean a stubbornness or an antagonistic spirit which refuses to see the right.

Another check-up is the constant search to realize how much one is building up a strong network of defenses which act to protect him from others, and incidently from himself.

Everyone is born into this world helpless and dependent. In order to survive each needs to be helped. The child grows up learning to turn to mother, not only for the comforts of physical help but for the more rewarding comfort of approval.

As each one grows older, he continues the search for approval from the widening group. He wants friends not only to like him, but to approve of what he does. In this approval he finds reassurance of his own worth.

So great is the human need for love and approval that one will even deceive himself, if necessary, rather than face the fact that he might not deserve it. Undisguised, one's behavior might not always merit approval. Everyone does things that are inconsiderate, unkind, downright cruel. But rather than face the self in an unkindly light, even to his own eyes, he unconsciously will protect the image of himself. Mortimer R. Feinberg, an industrial psychologist, has written an article which describes the forms of process that human beings use in this self-defense.

One is to rationalize — "did it because. . . " And then he goes on to provide what he thinks are good and substantial reasons for his behavior.

Another way is to project the thing that happened, disown the fault and see it as the other fellow's problem.

Another way is to displace. In this manner one blames someone else for his own faults which he can't accept.

Another method is to compensate by stretching self in one area when he had failed in another.

Feinberg gives a classic illustration of rationalization that a company's vice president, who was a former alcoholic, used. He expressed the way his mind deceived him as follows:

"When I was young and just out of college, I found the nicest people in bars. The men were all bright and the women charming. As I got older and started to the bar about four in the afternoon and stayed till two in the morning, I found the crowd was deteriorating! The most charming people never showed any more.

"I couldn't believe I was becoming an alcoholic, so one day I figured it all out. The bartenders were responsible. They weren't as intelligent as they used to be when I was younger. I, therefore, set about to correct the situation by spending time moving from bar to bar, giving the whisky tenders tests of general information. I felt certain that if bartenders were more interesting and informed then all the best people would return."[1]

The defenses that are set up in each individual serve two purposes, according to Mr. Feinberg. First, they represent an attempt to prove to others that a person is really fine and anything that he does wrong is done for the right reason. Second, and probably most important, these defenses help him to retain the image of himself as an important and productive person. So solid is the wall of defenses in most individuals that it becomes a barrier to self-knowledge.

In this process, defenses serve as a mask behind which one hides. But in addition, the road to self-knowledge is blocked by the fact that so much of one's behavior is controlled by his unconscious. Dr. Sigmund Freud, the father of modern psychoanalysis, was one of the first to understand the importance of the unconscious in determining behavior.

The safety devices operating from the unconscious work automatically. One has to be very skillful if he wants to sneak up on himself and take a quick look. How many times has one found himself doing the opposite of what he consciously intended to do?

As Ben Hecht observed in *Child of the Century:* "A wise man knows that he has only one enemy – himself. This is an enemy difficult to ignore and full of cunning. It assails one with doubts and fear. It always seeks to loosen and lead one away from one's goal. It is an enemy never to be forgotten but constantly outwitted."

[1] Mortimer R. Feinberg, *Nation's Business*

Feinberg suggests four methods for self-study.[1] In making these suggestions he encourages people to be sure that they call in expert help to penetrate the real depth. However, many of the instruments used by psychologists to probe into character can be adapted for use by the average person.

First is the autobiographical approach. Some people find it fruitful to probe their past, to uncover the critical incidents that helped determine what they are today. This is done by calling to mind the earliest memories about the important people in one's life.

By being honest in one's answers, the childhood conflicts with people will come to mind. Mature people can recognize the nature of the conflicts and understand now what they might not have seen at that period in their life. If one has this understanding, he is less likely to continue to act out his childhood conflicts in adult life.

Second is to note the extremes in one's life. The highs and lows, the extremes of one's emotions and feelings, often provide a clue to the core which lies hidden in the everyday controlled behavior. The unusual is, in effect, an exaggeration of the usual.

A person is not wise to dismiss the off-beat, unusual event as not typical.

As one makes a record of the unusual things in his reactions, he will find a good insight into himself. When he has enough of these separate items to form a picture, he can then look at them in relation to each other. Is there any common thread or pattern? Is there a special time of the day, a particular individual, a problem or situation which appears repeatedly? What is the individual role in each situation. Is one a by-stander or an active participant?

A third help in self-study is changing routine. Everyone tends to be blind to the familiar and accustomed things about him. Until a visit from a stranger jolts him into looking at his surroundings through another person's eyes, he may remain unaware of the most obvious facts. Most people lose themselves in the rush of daily pressures and become insensitive to their own reactions.

Since it is not possible for many people to go away for a long period and have time to think this through, it is best to take the procedure of measuring an entire day as if one is about to leave the job or the community. How would he act? What would he notice if he felt that he would never be in that place again? By changing his point of view for a day, one can often open his eyes and see himself and his behavior in a new light.

[1] *Ibid*, p. 78.

The fourth means of self-study is through cross-characterization. It is good for everyone to make a chart of the qualities of life and then have them checked by someone he works with, a friend, his wife, some other member of the family, and then for him to mark himself as he sees these qualities. Some qualities which should be included in the chart are: Kind, truthful, argumentative, eager, tense, understanding, thoughtful, humble, firm, optimistic, egotistical, shrewd, courageous, careful, selfish, impulsive, decisive, mature, devious, ambitious, imaginative, critical, fair-minded, easily-swayed, religious.

As you have read these pages, you have been given insight into your patterns of behavior and have learned that you must think your way through every stage and area of life as a football coach planning each play of the game. I pray you will let God guide your life to greater insights and fulfillment each day.